People in Mission

Series Preface

The **Global Voices** series takes the missiological work of writers who have written in their own language and makes this accessible to the English-speaking world through translation and republishing. The key principle here is that the translated work reflects the context, experience and thinking of the local context. In so doing, Regnum Books seeks to amplify voices less easily heard outside their own contexts. Work of this nature will make a significant contribution to the development of 'polycentric missiology'; namely, mission thinking and practice that truly reflects the contexts, concerns and contributions of the global church in all its rich diversity.

Series Editors

Paul Bendor-Samuel	Executive Director, Oxford Centre for Mission Studies
Mark Greenwood	BMS Overseas Team Leader for South America and Sub-Saharan Africa
Timóteo Carriker	Mission educator and consultant to the Brazilian Bible Society

People in Mission
An Autobiographical Reflection

Samuel Escobar Aguirre

Translated by Daniel John Clark

First published 2021 by Regnum Books International
Originally published as *Un pueblo en tiempo de misión*
2016, Centro de Investigaciones y Publicaciones (CENIP)
Ediciones Puma, Lima, Peru

Regnum is an imprint of the Oxford Centre for Mission Studies
St. Philip and St. James Church
Woodstock Road
Oxford OX2 6HR, UK
www.ocms.ac.uk/regnum

09 08 07 06 05 04 03 7 6 5 4 3 2 1

British Library Cataloguing in Publication Data
A catalogue record for this book is available from the British Library

ISBN: 978-1-5064-8399-3

eBook ISBN: 978-1-5064-8400-6

Typeset by Words by Design

The publication of this volume is made possible through the
financial assistance of **Evangelisches Missionswerk** and
BMS World Mission.

Distributed by 1517 Media in the US, Canada, India, and Brazil

CONTENTS

DEDICATION

I dedicate this book to Ruth Escobar Aguirre de Padilla, Débora Escobar Aguirre and Sara Dueñas Aguirre de Becerra, my sisters in the flesh and in the faith, all of whom labour in the service of the Lord Jesus Christ in our beloved Peru.

PREFACE

I have gathered the essays included in this book with a deep gratitude to the Lord for the way He has blessed Peru with a Baptist presence. I present the following pages as my small contribution to the 50th anniversary of the Peruvian Evangelical Baptist Convention (CEBP), aware of what it has meant for me to be part of the evangelical and Baptist movement in Peru and in the world.

The first part consists of an autobiographical chapter, written especially for this book. In the second part, I explore some aspects of Baptist missionary practice and theology. Ruth Escobar de Padilla distributed a prior version of chapters two and three in the form of lecture notes for her course on Baptist history at Lima Baptist Seminary in the second semester of 2009. These chapters have been revised carefully and updated for this current edition. The third part of this book is a collection of biographical sketches of Baptists whom I have met through the years of my pilgrimage, and who, in my opinion, illustrate the diverse ways Baptist Christians from different parts of the world live their faith and bear witness to their Lord. They first appeared in evangelical publications in Spain: the denominational magazine, El Eco Bautista, and the web page *Protestantedigital*, to which I regularly contribute. The two exceptions are chapter five, the biographical sketch of the Peruvian general, Ronald Román Caballero, and chapter eight, portraying the work of Margaret Swires, which were written especially for this present volume.

An author will always be in debt to many people no matter how small a book is. I want to thank the missionary Gary L. Crowell, whose master's thesis at Southwestern Baptist Theological Seminary of Texas, United States, is a valuable source of information and dates regarding Southern Baptist mission work in Peru. Likewise, I wish to thank Pastor Segundo Rosario Vásquez who years ago also wrote a thesis on Baptist history in Peru and was kind enough to give me a copy, and who has continued to help Peruvian Baptists recover their historical memory. I am especially grateful for the encouragement I received to write this book from pastors Pepe Flores, Jacob Padilla and Herbert García, and his wife Elena who with a group of experienced pastors and leaders, have been working for the recovery of the denomination's historical memory. As for my contribution to this process, I have written a few pages which, with a few modifications, I have included in my autobiographical account in the first chapter. I am grateful to Milagros Pélaez for having sent me historical and pedagogical material published by the Baptist associations of La Libertad and of Lima and Callao. I am also grateful to Tita and Janet Román for their precious assistance in preparing the biographical sketch of General Ronald Román Caballero.

I have a particularly great debt of gratitude to my sister Ruth Escobar de Padilla whose generous hospitality I always enjoy on my visits to Peru. In writing this book, we have spent many hours together remembering with gratitude our adolescence and youth, marked by the friendship and ministry of missionaries and pastors whom God used for our formation as Christians who seek to serve the Lord and his people.

I am grateful to Ediciones Puma, who have been publishing various works on evangelical history in Peru, for having published the Spanish original of this present volume, which I published with the hope that it will contribute to allowing Peruvian Baptists and evangelicals to know their history and to strengthen themselves on the biblical and theological foundation of their faith and testimony, for the greater glory of God.

For this edition in English I want to express my deep gratitude to missionary Daniel Clark from the Baptist Seminary in Lima for his excellent work of translation. He has evidently grasped the pedagogical intention of my effort in this book and has communicated it clearly to the English reader. *Soli Deo Gloria.*

Valencia, December 2020.

PART ONE

My Baptist Pilgrimage

1: MY BAPTIST PILGRIMAGE

I consider it a special privilege to have been invited to participate with my Peruvian Baptist brothers and sisters in the celebration of the first fifty years of the Peruvian Evangelical Baptist Convention (CEBP). This celebration is evidence of the Lord's desire to bless the work of sowing the Gospel and planting churches which started in 1950 and offers the opportunity to remember the journey travelled so far with an eye to the future. This present work seeks to contribute to the recovery of historical memory, a task a new generation of Peruvian Baptists needs to carry out.

I wish to emphasise that this work is mainly autobiographical and does not seek to be an academic historical essay. I write it to share and reflect on my experiences among Baptists. Nonetheless, my reflection, when necessary, makes use of missiological concepts and criteria as these tools help us better understand the meaning and value of personal experiences. Also, I occasionally provide historical summaries which help to understand my personal pilgrimage. These summaries are based on my own memories, at times in the form of notes in personal journals and also on information regarding minutes, dates and events gathered by Gary Crowell in his master's thesis.[1] In this introductory work, I will limit myself to the first decade of Baptist history in Peru (1950–1960) as in 1960 I left with my wife for Argentina to carry out inter-denominational mission work among university students in Argentina, and other countries. Since then, although I have maintained a continuous interest, I have only been able to follow the advance of Baptist work in our homeland from afar.

My Baptist pilgrimage started at the age of seventeen on the last Sunday of August in 1951 when I visited, for the first time, Ebenezer Baptist Church in Miraflores and experienced a warm, fraternal welcome from pastors David Oates and Antonio Gamarra. I was taken to the church by Jaime Dávila, my roommate in the student lodgings we rented in the centre of Lima, two blocks away from the central campus of San Marcos University.

---

[1] Gary L. Crowell, "A History of Southern Baptist Mission Work in Peru 1950-1995", Master's thesis in Missiology, Southwestern Baptist Theological Seminary, April 1996. See comments at the end of this chapter.

Jaime Dávila had travelled from Puno and I had come from Arequipa to Lima to study at the University in 1951. We met at the Peruvian Evangelical Church (IEP) at Calle Mandamientos (now Maranata on Avenida Brasil). This church did not have a minister at the time so, although we wanted to participate actively in church life, we missed effective pastoral support and good preaching. I had grown up and been discipled in the IEP of Arequipa by missionaries Iza Elder and Susan May Pritchard and received biblical instruction at Latin Link's International School. Sporadic visits from missionaries, such as Leslie Hoggarth, Alex Jardine and David Milnes, led me to appreciate good biblical exposition and pastoral counselling. Jaime had encountered the Gospel in Puno, thanks to the presence and ministry of Irish Baptists, especially Samuel Sloan. Therefore, when he heard that a Baptist church had opened in Miraflores, he encouraged me to visit it with him. What we both appreciated in that emerging church was precisely pastoral guidance and good preaching.

We were welcomed warmly and encouraged to collaborate in the work. This led us to ask for baptism and soon we received careful baptismal instruction from pastors Oates and Gamarra. Jaime and I were baptised on the 27th October 1951 by Pastor Oates. *This initial experience and my journey of more than sixty years in various countries confirm for me an important principle: churches which grow and carry out their missionary labour need to be welcoming churches. This requires both pastoral initiative and congregational effort to ensure that churches truly become welcoming communities.*

What I most appreciated from the Baptist distinctives we were taught before baptism was the vision of the church as a community of believers, and the fact that baptism should come after a confession of faith. I was also attracted by the teaching that church government should be congregational rather than episcopal; that is, it should not be linked to a hierarchy which in extreme cases considers itself infallible. I had already pretty much developed my own convictions regarding the authority of the Bible, individual salvation through faith in the expiatory death of Christ rather than one's own works, and the work of God in creation during my time at the IEP. I had also developed my own convictions regarding the person of Jesus Christ and the work of the Holy Spirit.

This church in Miraflores was the first church started by Southern Baptists in Peru only a few weeks before our baptism. It was the first of those churches that would, years later, in January 1966, form the Peruvian Evangelical Baptist Convention (CEBP). Many of these churches were a result of the missionary impulse which followed the arrival of missionaries sent by the Southern Baptist Convention of the United States from 1950 onwards. Nonetheless, these churches were not the only Baptist presence in Peru. I believe it is beneficial and necessary to make a brief reference to those Baptists who came before or after those who formed the CEBP.

Baptist Presence in Peru

The great pioneer Diego Thomson [James Thomson, known as Diego Thomson in Spanish speaking countries], acknowledged as the forerunner of evangelical presence in Peru, was a Baptist. He arrived in Callao on 28th June 1822 and established himself in Lima where he worked until 5 September 1824, when he left for Colombia.[2] Thomson was a representative of the British and Foreign Schools Society, an educational organisation based on the Lancasterian or Monitorial System which, at the time, was considered the most advanced pedagogical approach. Thomson's friendship with the Liberator José de San Martín, as well as his previous experience in Argentina and Chile, led San Martín to invite Thomson to organise popular education and teacher training in the new Peruvian republic. For this reason, Thomson is regarded as the founder of the first teacher training school in Peru. He was also linked to the British and Foreign Bible Society and thus carried out the distribution of Bibles whilst undertaking his responsibilities as an educator.

Thomson had been born into a Presbyterian home in Scotland but through the influence of the Haldane brothers who followed Baptist principles, he had a conversion experience in his youth. Letters and other literature from this period refer to Thomson as Reverend, which suggests that he was probably ordained as a Baptist minister, and the Scottish Baptists recognise him as one of their main historical figures. Nonetheless, Thomson believed that the distribution of Bibles in Peru would bring revival and reform within the Catholic church and did not adopt a missionary agenda of planting Baptist churches in the country. Thomson managed to enlist the support of some priests interested in the Bible, the most significant being José Francisco Navarrete who continued Thomson's educational labour and Bible promotion.

There is no record of the presence of any other Baptist missionary in Peru in the 19th century after Thomson's departure. The Irish Baptists, associated with the Baptist Foreign Mission formed by the Irish Baptist Union in 1924, arrived well into the 20th century.[3] The Irish Baptists decided to focus their missionary efforts on the Latin American indigenous population which they considered to be a group with tremendous material and spiritual needs. In time, they concentrated on two countries: Argentina and Peru. In Argentina, they focused their activity in the city of Rosario where five churches had emerged through the initiative of an Irish layman. In Peru, they initially decided to send missionaries

---

[2] The most complete study about Thomson is Donald Mitchell, "The Evangelical Contribution of James Thomson to South American Life 1818-1825", unpublished doctoral thesis, Princeton Theological Seminary, 1972.
[3] Information regarding Irish Baptists comes from Andrew Reid, *By Divine Coincidence: A History of Irish Baptist Foreign Mission* (Belfast: Association of Baptist Churches in Ireland, 2000).

to Urubamba in Cusco. The first Irish Baptist missionary, Robert Bennett, arrived at the Peruvian port of Mollendo in August 1928. He was followed a year later by William Creighton. After a period of exploration and consultation with other missionaries, the Irish decided to concentrate their work in the three southern regions of Tacna, Puno and Moquegua.

Other Protestant missions already established in Peru assigned this area to the Irish Baptists. Among these missions was the British Evangelical Union of South America, now known as Latin Link, with whom the Irish had a friendly relationship. Through an agreement advised by the Evangelical Congress of Panama in 1916, Protestant missionaries in Peru upheld a system of consultation and cooperation and avoided sending new missionaries to those regions where other denominations were already working to avoid duplication. For this reason, the Nazarenes went to the North (Lambayeque, La Libertad), the Presbyterians to the North-East (Amazon), although they founded a school in Lima, the Methodists to the centre of the country (Lima, Huancayo), and the Evangelical Union to the South (Cusco, Arequipa, Ica). As the Evangelical Union's work became concentrated in Cusco and Arequipa, they left Puno, Moquegua and Tacna without an evangelical missionary presence. This consultation and cooperation laid the foundation for the formation of the National Evangelical Council of Peru (CONEP) in 1940. Nonetheless, the first Southern Baptist missionary to arrive in Peru in 1950, Clifford Belle Oates, did not accept this policy of assigning mission fields and followed the strategy that he, and his mission board, believed to be more appropriate, without consulting any other church or denomination.

The Irish Baptists had little success in the south of Peru, notwithstanding the intense and dedicated labour of their missionaries which was replicated in the sacrificial evangelistic dedication of the Peruvian believers in their churches. Further ahead, they entered a cooperative effort with Argentinian Baptists. Well-known pastors and evangelists from the city of Rosario, such as Rodolfo Zambrano and Orlando Ávalos, cooperated with the Irish, spending a few years of missionary service in Tacna and neighbouring areas. This work would have repercussions later in other parts of Peru. In this way, Ángel Murillo, who became treasurer of the First Baptist Church of Lima in the 1960s, came to faith in Tacna, attracted to the football team which the Argentinian Zambrano organised to take the gospel to the youth of Tacna. Similarly, the above-mentioned engineer, Jaime Dávila, who would become an active member of Ebenezer Church in Miraflores, converted in Puno through the ministry of an Irish Baptist missionary.

In the Peruvian jungle, especially in Iquitos, some independent Baptist missionaries carried out evangelism and church planting. These independent efforts were normally linked to fundamentalist churches in the United States and avoided cooperation with other denominations and evangelical churches. In 1960, missionaries from Baptist Mid-Missions, an organisation associated with the fundamentalist Carl McIntire's International Council of Christian Churches arrived in Peru. In 1965, when the CONEP assembly and a pastor's retreat organised by World Vision took place in Huampaní, these missionaries organised a rival fundamentalist event which had little significance. The Biblical Baptist Churches derived from this effort have continued to evolve in subsequent years.

Initial Advance of the Southern Baptists

The first Southern Baptist missionary to establish himself in Peru was Clifford Belle Oates, soon known as David, who arrived in Lima with his wife Marion Davis Oates on 13th September 1950. He was a dynamic man, an enthusiastic preacher and a very able sportsman with an entrepreneurial vision and spirit. He rented a house to start having meetings at 401 Angamos Avenue, in the residential district of Miraflores, and rented the house next door to live with his family. He contacted Dr Herbert Money, secretary of the National Evangelical Council of Peru (CONEP) who instructed Oates that CONEP had designated him to evangelise in the southern jungle region, close to the borders with Brazil and Bolivia. Oates replied that he had his own plans and was going to start work in the Lima district of Miraflores.

Soon after settling in, Oates invited the Argentinian pastor, Antonio Gamarra, to collaborate in Peru. Gamarra and his wife, Mercedes Baldomir, arrived in Peru on 27th February 1951. Both had studied at the International Baptist Seminary of Buenos Aires and had worked in Ecuador and Bolivia. Gamarra was an excellent preacher, a tireless worker and a devoted Christian labourer willing to carry out door-to-door evangelism. His wife sang hymns in a very attractive way as she had a magnificent voice and was able to accompany herself on the piano. Oates and Gamarra started in Miraflores with a visitation plan and on 18th March 1951, carried out their first service at the location rented on Angamos Avenue. A few months later, on 19th August 1951, what would become the first Baptist church was organised with nine members, some of whom came from other evangelical denominations. As time went by, the church took the name Ebenezer of Miraflores.

Robert Harris and his wife, Mary Lillian, arrived as missionaries in Peru on 31st October 1951. These missionaries stood out for the way they cultivated a deep and disciplined spiritual life and had a special way with people that attracted the respect and sympathy of Peruvian believers. Oates and Harris, along with their wives, organised themselves as the Baptist Mission in Peru and worked together, being the only Baptist missionaries until the arrival of Randall Sledge in 1956. Oates and Harris formed a team with Antonio Gamarra and his wife. In 1954, they were joined by Alejandro Tuesta, a Presbyterian pastor from the jungle, a very good teacher and preacher who had explicitly decided to adopt Baptist theology and practice. The Cuban pastor, Luis Manuel Agüero Serrano, and his wife Julia Remedios de Agüero, joined the team in February 1955 through Oates' invitation. Agüero had an engaging, extrovert personality and was an expert in Christian education, as well as in organising Sunday Schools and youth groups, while his wife had a degree in teaching. The Baptist Mission provided financial support for pastors Gamarra, Tuesta and Agüero.

As the church in Miraflores grew and advanced under the leadership of David Oates, Pastor Antonio Gamarra decided to explore the possibility of opening another church close to the centre of Lima. He started a visitation plan in the area surrounding the strategic corner of Wilson (now Garcilaso de la Vega) Avenue on 28th July and established contacts in the continuous and patient labour of personal evangelism. Consequently, in November 1952 the Gamarra couple and six others organised themselves as the First Baptist Church of Lima in a rented location on the second floor of a home in Block 17 of Wilson Avenue in Lima. Gamarra's talent for clear and profound systematic expository preaching was accompanied by his wife's talent and expertise in the careful use of music.[4] At the same time, Oates and Gamarra managed to negotiate a fifteen-minute slot on Sunday evenings with the director of Victoria Radio for a programme that included preaching and music. The proximity of the radio studio to the church building allowed for some fruitful contacts to be established.

Harris had met people living in the district of Lince and followed up these meetings with visits and prayer. This work began first as a congregation of Ebenezer Church in Miraflores but in May 1953, became an independent church with Harris as pastor. In this way, the Baptist work which had carried out its first public service in March 1951, by 1953 had three churches which remained the foundation and basis for Baptist growth in Peru.

Soon the work would spread from Lima on a national scale. Contacts established by the First Church with a group of evangelical Christians in Arequipa, the White City, resulted in the formation of the First Baptist Church in Arequipa, which was organised in November 1954. As I spent the summer months in Arequipa, from the summer of 1955 onwards I was able to collaborate in the initial stages of the church, preaching and teaching alongside Vicente Rosas, a young man from Arequipa who had converted to the gospel in Lima, and the Vilca family. Together with Vicente, we organised a personal development course which started with a systematic study of John A. Broadus' book, *On the Preparation and Delivery of Sermons*.

In the city of Trujillo, there was a Baptist church which had been founded by independent Baptist missionary, Oliver Bell. He contacted the Southern Baptist missionaries asking to join their work. This led to the emergence of the Central Baptist Church of Trujillo. In his unpublished autobiographical account, Pastor

---

[4] Translator's note: Lima is both the name of the whole city and of the district in the centre of the city. Hence the church founded by Gamarra became the "First Baptist Church of Lima" even though the church in Miraflores was the first Baptist church established in Lima (whole city).

Herbert García has described his conversion experience in that church, a consequence of ten years of intense evangelist labour by Oliver Bell who, from 1945 onwards, travelled the Department of La Libertad on horseback preaching the Gospel.[5]

Entry into the Baptist World Family

In July 1953, the World Baptist Youth Congress took place in Rio de Janeiro, Brazil. David Oates informed the young people at Ebenezer Baptist Church of Miraflores that he had received an invitation for Peruvian Baptists to send delegates to this conference, and that the mission was willing to help with the travel costs of one delegate.[6] After considering this proposal, the majority of young people chose me to be a delegate at the Congress. Thus, in July 1953, I took a Braniff Airways flight from Lima to Rio de Janeiro and had the privilege of participating in the Congress, which was a most valuable experience and allowed me to get to know Baptists from other Latin-American countries, and from the whole world. For the first time, Peruvian Baptists were represented at a global gathering. In this Congress, I met the Argentinians Jacobo Vartanián, Samuel Libert and Arnoldo Canclini, the Brazilians Werner Kaschel and Joarés de Azevedo, the Venezuelan Neftalí Prato, and Pedro Bonet from Spain. I developed friendships with some of them and I still remember the clear and pertinent exposition of the Book of Acts by Dr Culbert Rutenberg, a Northern Baptist and professor at Eastern Baptist Seminary in Philadelphia, United States, where I would end up teaching in 1985.

On my return flight to Peru, I passed through Argentina where I arrived on 24th July 1953 and stayed for a week in Buenos Aires at the Baptist Seminary. This allowed me to meet and talk with Argentinian and Bolivian seminary students, and I was able to become aware of aspects of Baptist church life in Argentina.

I also had the opportunity, in Buenos Aires, to meet the Presbyterian theologian, Juan A. Mackay, who had been a missionary in Peru between 1916 and 1924 and had founded the San Andrés College. He was in Buenos Aires at the Carnahan Conference in the Theological Faculty, an ecumenical institution which would later become known as ISEDET. I had read two books by Mackay which had decisively influenced my formation – *The Meaning of Life* and *Preface to Christian Theology*. With the assistance of someone at the Baptist

---

[5] Herbert García, "Material Biográfico", unpublished material shared by the author.
[6] Translator's note: IMB (International Mission Board) work in Peru is known simply as the "Misión Extrenjera" (foreign mission, due to its legal registration) or simply "la misión" (the mission) or "la misión bautista" (the Baptist Mission). This is reflected in the original text.

Seminary who took pity on me, I was able to ask over the telephone for an interview with Dr Mackay. He granted me the interview and the experience would leave a profound legacy on my life.

I am still moved when I remember the experience of being received by the Scottish teacher for a long and, for me, precious hour. I asked Mackay many questions that day. I remember his books and the careful attention with which he listened to me that afternoon, with his blue eyes gazing intently at me which encouraged me to ask him all kinds of questions. Mackay talked with me about Christian theology, ecumenism, evangelical convictions and his book, *The Other Spanish Christ*. At the end of our conversation, he asked me with much interest about the APRA political leader, Victor Raúl Haya de la Torre, who was at that time in asylum at the Colombian Embassy, a victim of the oligarchic, military regime of General Manuel Apolinario Odría. Being able to move from the riches of theology to the contingencies of current history was precisely what I admired in Mackay and made me enjoy that afternoon. My heart still burns at the memory.[7]

I can affirm with certainty that this immersion in the Congress, meeting so many people and receiving reports of Baptist work in other parts of the world gave me an understanding of Baptist reality which, until then, I had not received from the missionaries and pastors with whom I had been receiving my formation. Reflecting on this experience, I realised that there were ways of being a Baptist which were different to those represented by the North American missionaries in Peru, and I found them attractive.

The fact that I could speak English was also a great help in my Baptist formation as whenever an important Baptist arrived in Peru, David Oates would ask me to look after them and take them around Lima for a few hours. Thus, I was able to meet Fred Townley Lord, president of the Baptist World Alliance, and the Baptist historian and writer, E. H. Robertson, both British. In 1956, I had the privilege of acting as a guide for Kenneth Scott Latourette, professor at Yale University, the greatest Baptist historian, who was visiting Lima on his way to Buenos Aires to carry out the Carnahan Lectures at the Union Seminary of Buenos Aires.

The different national backgrounds of Oates and Harris in comparison to Gamarra and Agüero led to different perspectives on what should be emphasised in the new Baptist work. For example, the Argentinian Baptists came from work started by Swiss and British Baptists with a strong emphasis on home visits and quality preaching. In comparison, the Cuban Baptists were similar to the American Baptists in their emphasis on adapting Christian educational organisations for children, youth and women to the Cuban reality.

---

[7] I have studied the life and work of Mackay in my book, *In Search of Christ in Latin America* (Downers Grove: Inter Varsity Press, 2019).

Baptist Educational and Youth Work

As I point out in the second chapter of this book, a key principle in Protestant missionary practice has been to link evangelism and church planting with educational work, opening schools and colleges. The Southern Baptists tried to follow this principle in Peru and the Baptist Mission started two primary schools in April 1954 at the beginning of the school year. Colegio Angamos was opened in Miraflores using rooms at Ebenezer Baptist Church. At that time, I was in the third year of my studies in the Educational Faculty of San Marcos University and was one of the those invited to help, being nominated to teach the first year of primary school. On the other hand, Alejandro Tuesta, a licensed teacher and pastor, became director of Colegio San Juan at a location rented by the Mission for the church in the district of Lince, on Avenida Militar, a few metres from Lince's main square. Colegio Redentor started functioning in 1955 at the First Baptist Church.

In February 1953, through the enthusiastic initiative of David Oates, a youth retreat took place on a beach near Mala, south of Lima. Organisers found a favourable location near a wall of rock, where they set up tents to function as a dormitory, improvised latrines and erected a roofed shed to function as a kitchen and dining room. The programme included sports and entertainment, music, time for rest, sermons and biblical exposition. I found that first retreat a novelty and enjoyed it very much as I had never encountered something similar in my evangelical experience. *The possibility of staying together for many days with pastors and preachers, with time for services, teaching, reflection, rest and recreation in a relaxed environment, had a permanent impact on my development. Many of the first Peruvian Baptist pastors, such as Jacobo Padilla, Julio Villar, David Trigoso and Fernando Cárdenas, received their ministerial call at the retreat. Through the decades in my own ministry in churches and organisations, retreats have had an important and decisive role, especially in training programmes.* Mala beach, where we carried out this first retreat, and the surrounding areas were later used by the Peruvian Scripture Union which built a retreat centre in Kauai.

In 1954, the Baptist Mission made a significant investment to start a Baptist ministry among students. Oates invited AnneLu Bagby, a young woman and daughter of a well-known Baptist missionary family in Brazil, to work in the Mission's office and on the project of forming a Baptist student centre. University students from Ebenezer Church of Miraflores, such as Oscar Ríos, Javier del Águila and myself, worked actively and the Baptist Student Circle was formed. The Circle met in a room in the Mission's office on Antonio Miró Quesada street in the centre of Lima, which had a table-tennis table, games and facilities to prepare coffee and juice. For some meetings, up to thirty university students gathered at this location, about five blocks from the central building of San Marcos University. Due to internal politics, the Mission decided to close the project at the start of 1955 without offering any explanation to participants.

AnneLu Bagby returned to the United States and the university students were left without a location, no secretarial assistance and little enthusiasm to carry on.

Slightly disappointed with the ups and downs of mission politics, I started to actively participate in a self-sustaining project convened by Ruth Siemens, an American educationalist who worked at the American Roosevelt School in San Isidro. Evangelical university students would meet at the homes of missionaries or professional friends contributing with our time, enthusiasm and some money. It was the start of the University Bible Circle, which was inter-denominational and allowed Baptist, Methodist, IEP [Peruvian Evangelical Church], Presbyterian and Pentecostal university students to get to know each other. In this circle, I learnt the discipline of daily and regular Bible reading and prayer in support of Christian discipleship. The Circle was able to have an impact on the University and in time, this led to the formation of the Association of Evangelical College Groups in Peru (AGEUP), which in 2013 celebrated fifty years of organisation.

The missionaries did not look favourably on my participation in inter-denominational initiatives and believed it was necessary to protect the Baptist identity with a separatist attitude. My participation in the aforementioned Rio Congress, my readings and the fact that I had grown up in a different denominational environment led me to believe that the missionaries' strict denominationalism was not appropriate for countries in which evangelicals are a minority and in environments such as the university, which are far more critical of divisions among evangelicals. Since then, I have maintained my Baptist identity as a member of different Baptist churches and been linked in different ways to the Baptist World Alliance. At the same time, I have worked in different inter-denominational environments, such as the Latin American Theological Fraternity, the Lausanne Movement, the United Bible Societies and the International Fellowship of Evangelical Students.

Baptist Missionary Strategy

Both Jaime Dávila and I sought to understand Baptist doctrine and practice. Due to our prior experience in other churches, we were also interested in understanding the missionary strategy proposed by missionaries who started the Baptist work. From observing lectures by Oates and Gamarra, and engaging in lengthy conversations with them, we became convinced that these pioneers had a clear missionary strategy. As far as we could tell as young Christians, this strategy could be summarised in five main points:

a) *To seek to evangelise the upper and middle classes,* a goal which other denominations had apparently not achieved in Peru. For this reason, they chose to start in the district of Miraflores and sought to put together a team containing able and noteworthy personnel, such as Pastor Gamarra and his wife. David Oates, who had experienced significant success as a tennis player at Baylor University, became a member of Las Terrazas Tennis Club, using his sporting experience to form relationships with well-off young people in Miraflores. Nonetheless, despite a few sporadic visits from the residents of Miraflores, most people who came and remained in the church were from poorer neighbourhoods, such as Surquillo and Santa Cruz. Once more, one could perceive that Lima's upper classes were still not open to the Gospel.

b) *Work creatively among young people.* As indicated, Baptists organised the first youth retreat in Peru at Mala beach and this was soon imitated by other churches and denominations. At the same time, Oates emphasised sports and the participation of Baptist youth in evangelical tournaments. Concerning student ministry, I concluded that a contextual and inter-denominational approach was more appropriate than a denominational one.

c) *Raising the social and economic status of pastors*, starting with foreign aid to pay decent and adequate wages. The idea was that through intense and practical teaching on stewardship, this initial funding would allow churches to become self-sustaining. The goal was also to offer quality theological education due to the conviction that those who carried out pastoral and teaching ministry in churches needed to be adequately prepared to do so. Initially, some young men were encouraged to prepare themselves outside of Peru and received financial support. In 1959, the Lima Baptist Theological Institute began with nine students. I believe that Baptists contributed to raising awareness regarding theological education in Peru. In comparison, the issue of pastoral wages became an area of controversy when a crisis soon emerged.

d) *To build adequate places for church services and pay what was required to do so.* This was carried out from the outset and in less than five years, there was a beautiful and functional temple in Miraflores, and investments had been made for properties for other churches. However, the legal ownership of the property purchased on Paseo Colón Avenue, near the centre of Lima, became one of the reasons for the 1956 crisis.

e) *Reaching other cities according to an order of importance*, stimulating lay workers for this extension. This led to positive results as missionaries were willing to move and live in different places and there was enthusiastic participation by Peruvian Christians who managed to attract new believers, and some independent churches joined the Baptist work. It is hard to establish the extent to which the first missionaries sought to understand the national situation and learn from other denominations, and their methodology in developing their strategy. My own impression is that Oates did not pay much attention to this. Nonetheless, in this first stage a generation of young leaders from other denominations, such as the Presbyterians (especially the Rios and Rojas families from Rioja and Moyobamba), the Nazarenes (especially the Arana and Bullón families from Chiclayo and Monsefú), and the Peruvian Evangelical Church (especially the Trigoso and Escobar families from Lima and Arequipa), were attracted by different aspects of Baptist strategy and in time adopted Baptist principles out of conviction.

Gary Crowell's historical thesis suggests that the first generation of missionaries perceived their work as establishing Southern Baptist Churches in Peru.[8] The Southern Baptists are a denomination with a strong regional identity in the United States. Some of these characteristics, such as supporting and defending racial segregation, reflect typical characteristics and values of the Southern states of that country and neither represent biblical teaching, nor the Baptist theological heritage. Missionary work in the long term would need to seek the emergence and growth of Peruvian Baptist Churches with their own Biblical, theological and cultural identity. Realising this requires time, experience and spiritual growth, only mature missionaries reach this understanding. Crowell also indicates that these missionaries wanted their churches to grow through evangelism and not by attracting those from other denominations.[9]

Initial Assessment by the End of 1955

Gary Crowell provides an assessment of what had been achieved by 1955, based on data from mission minutes. After five years of labour, there were five churches led by Peruvian or Latin American pastors and missionaries, with a total of 198 members, fifteen Sunday schools with about a thousand students, and three primary schools with 178 students. Churches also enthusiastically followed an educational programme in organisations for women and young people, and the churches of Lima, Trujillo and Arequipa expressed their missionary and evangelistic vocation in the form of various efforts to plant new churches.[10] The numbers themselves are not able to convey how those of us who participated in those initial years shared a rich, fraternal, spiritual experience.

The significant growth of the Southern Baptists in their first five years of presence in Peru was thus a consequence of the Mission's intense investment of economic resources to provide experienced pastors and good Spanish speaking preachers and evangelists, many of them foreigners; well located, adequate church buildings; camps for young people and children and primary schools, some of them located near the churches. Missionary strategy was also able to mobilise believers who were united in participating in door-to-door evangelism so that churches had a missionary and evangelistic spirit. New believers were recent converts and followed a methodical and carefully prepared evangelistic plan.

It is important to emphasise that both the missionaries, Oates and Harris, and the pastors Gamarra and Agüero, offered a personal example, moving beyond

---

[8] Gary L. Crowell, op. cit., 12.
[9] Ibid., 9-11.
[10] Ibid., 17.

theory, of the importance of home-to-home visitations and sharing evangelistic materials and invitations to church services. They also taught the importance of prayer as a preparation in the home and in the church. I firmly believe that any fruits that were obtained in those first years were a consequence of the Holy Spirit answering our prayers, giving us the strength and enthusiasm to go onto the streets with the message of the Gospel. I recall that when we inaugurated the first church building of Ebenezer Baptist Church of Miraflores, we held a prayer service which lasted until midnight in which the Holy Spirit touched our hearts; people dedicated their lives further to God and asked one another for forgiveness, leading to reconciliation. We were pastored by people who in their own lives modelled what they taught us and stimulated us to imitate them.

The evangelistic spirit of churches and their pastoral labour encouraged persons from other denominations to join in the first years. Luis Manuel Agüero and his wife Julia, from Cuba, provided an excellent contribution in the field of Christian education, youth organisations and pastoral care. Pastor Alejandro Tuesta brought excellent expository preaching from his Presbyterian past. Thus, the first three churches, Miraflores, Lima and Lince had a constant and effective pastoral presence. Therefore, the first five years of flourishing were not only a consequence of the mission's economic resources but also due to the presence of well-prepared missionaries and pastors who, on the whole, knew how to treat Peruvians with respect, appreciation and vision, and with this managed to disciple and mobilise churches.

It is important to emphasise that in these first years of Baptist work the first generation of ministers and pastors Oates, Harris, Gamarra and Agüero, along with their wives, opened their homes to Peruvian youth for visits, meals and games. This allowed for lengthy conversations concerning faith and pastoral advice, which was decisive in the initial stage of the work. Unfortunately, many subsequent missionaries did not cultivate this; this spirit was lost when conflicts started and attitudes hardened. As we study Christian mission, it is possible to observe that hospitality has been an important element in missionary advance since the Book of Acts in New Testament times.[11]

Although there was, at this time, no organisation which represented all Baptist churches, nonetheless, various united meetings held on special occasions allowed one to feel that there was a Baptist people in Peru which was growing despite its ups and downs. I especially recall the great evangelistic campaigns with the Argentinian pastor, Rodolfo Zambrano and the Cuban pastor, Doctor Luis Manuel González Peña.

Both modelled a preaching style which balances deep biblical content with adequate contextual communication. We took González Peña to give

---

[11] An excellent study about this issue is Christine D. Pohl, *Making Room. Recovering Hospitality as a Christian Tradition* (Grand Rapids: Eerdmans, 1999).

conferences at San Marcos University, followed by question-and-answer sessions. Many university students came to faith in Christ and in other cases, those who were struggling with their faith were strengthened to offer a more public testimony in classrooms and they became active in the University Bible Circle.

A Time of Crisis

1956 can be described as the year of crisis for Baptists in Peru. As has happened continuously throughout history, since the first Christian church in Jerusalem (Acts 6:1–7), the crisis originated in the practical consequences of different attitudes towards the material infrastructure of land, buildings, salaries and economical resources which are required to take forward the apostolic task of evangelisation and church planting. The Peruvian Baptist crisis of 1956 is directly related to issues surrounding the material infrastructure that is essential for mission. My narrative of this stage in my pilgrimage is based upon notes in my diaries from these months and my memories of those events. I have also had conversations with pastors Herbert García and Jacob Padilla. Gary Crowell's thesis offers valuable information concerning events and dates from the Mission's own archives and internal correspondence. Pastor Herbert García has written an autobiographical 23-page manuscript with the title *Biographical Material,* which he has generously let me use.

At this time, there was still no full religious freedom in Peru nor was there a clear legal framework for the new emerging churches. Nonetheless, the Baptist Mission still needed to acquire a juridical status which allowed it to manage economic resources, financially support ministers, and buy land destined for church buildings, as well as run schools and educational centres. Hence, what Peruvian Baptists would call missionary support for workers for the Mission in its relationship with Peruvian authorities became workers' wages. In a subtle way, the fraternal relationships between missionaries and national workers would transform themselves into labour relationships between bosses and employees.

In March 1953, Oates obtained support from the Richmond Baptist Mission Board to purchase land destined for the construction of a building for the Ebenezer Baptist Church of Miraflores at 799 Coronel Inclán Avenue. Whilst the building work took place, the church set up a tent and carried out evangelistic campaigns. There were difficulties in obtaining building permission from the Municipality and this required much persistence and diplomacy from Oates. Finally, in June 1954, the Baptists in Lima were able to rejoice at the inauguration of the new church building of Ebenezer Baptist Church in Miraflores. The Mission also acquired a home for missionaries at 215 Enrique Meiggs Street in Miraflores where the Oates family and subsequently others lived. It would later become a guest house for the mission. In June 1954, funding was obtained to purchase land to build a retreat centre in Santa Eulalia, 48 kilometres east from Lima along the Central Highway.

By the end of 1955, the Mission had developed a financial plan to present to the churches. Until then, the Mission had been paying the salaries and benefits of pastors Gamarra, Tuesta and Agüero directly. The new plan was that the funds for these salaries would be given to each church which would be responsible for paying the ministers. Furthermore, the plan was for the Mission's financial aid to reduce by 10% each year so that the churches could become self-sustaining in ten years. This plan assumed that each church would have a finance commission and would present a yearly budget to the Mission including all their expenses. Up to this point, churches had been instructed concerning stewardship and believers were giving regularly with an appropriate attitude. Nonetheless, the Mission's plan was not realistic and for many reasons the pastors opposed it. An important aspect of the plan was that the churches which used Mission properties had to maintain their Baptist identity and have their missionary methodologies and approaches approved by the Mission.

The Mission had purchased a property at 209 Paseo Colón in Lima where it planned to build a property for the First Baptist Church. This was an old, luxurious residence on a strategic, prestigious street, a short distance from where the church was meeting on Wilson Avenue. Both the church and the Mission agreed that the site would be used as student accommodation until the church building was constructed and over a dozen students ended up living there. I was blessed to share a room at this site for various months.

Pastor Antonio Gamarra was convinced that this site belonged to the First Baptist Church, not the Mission. His understanding was that the donors had given it to the church, even though at that time the church did not have a legal identity allowing it to possess and administer properties. Consequently, under Gamarra's guidance, the membership of the First Church left the Wilson Avenue site and occupied the property at 209 Paseo Colón. This resulted in a confrontation which became worse as missionaries followed the advice of a lawyer, whose surname was Ribeyro, to establish their right to property which Gamarra had questioned. On 4th November 1956, Pastor Antonio Gamarra was forced to resign his pastoral functions. The Mission had forced him to choose between resigning or being fired and asked him to abandon Peru. Gamarra sought to sue the mission in the Peruvian courts over various subjects. Baptists in the Miraflores and Lince churches observed this fast deterioration of relationships with sorrow. I recall that Pastor Agüero advised Gamarra not to continue with his legal case and I also dialogued with Gamarra and his wife to this effect, but they carried on with their legal demands. Even though pastors Agüero and Tuesta did not agree with Gamarra over taking the Mission to court, they sided with him over the Mission's demands that he abandon the country. Eventually, Gamarra returned to Argentina. Gamarra's resignation and the family's departure to Argentina was a hard blow for the membership of the First Church.

A new missionary couple, Randall and Dorothy Sledge, arrived in Lima on 14th April 1956 amid this tense confrontation. In October, Roy and Marta Chamblee arrived and in December, Bryan and Vickey Brasington. All of them soon became involved in the confrontation and adopted the antagonistic attitude of the Mission, ignorant of the good quality of relationship in the first years. Sadly, the conflict between Gamarra and the Mission started to poison the opinions and attitudes of believers in other churches, leading to polarization in favour or against the missionaries. The Mission's attitude was increasingly one of suspicion and distrust, and it started to put pastors Agüero and Tuesta under pressure. Personally, as a young 21-year-old, it was a sad experience for me to see older persons, pastors and missionaries whom I admired very much face each other as enemies, and use legal arguments rather than fraternal dialogue. Nonetheless, during this period, Robert Harris and his wife's respect and manners in their personal attitudes and relationships provided an example of Christian charity, which left a profound legacy in my memory.

My years of Baptist and evangelical militancy have taught me that sincere and timely dialogue, based on mutual fraternal appreciation, is always helpful when there are differences of opinion. It is easy to fall into the temptation of resorting to confrontation and quarrelling as the only way to resolve differences or plan shared actions, and this always ends up as a source of scandal for those on the outside and demoralisation for those on the inside. The Epistles of Paul, Peter and John repeatedly insist that love and fraternal appreciation are a decisive mark of Christian identity. They also insist that we should forgive one another. Being able to recognise our own errors and to have patience with others is an important sign of maturity in Christ.

Pastor Luis Manuel Agüero resigned from his work with the Mission in November of 1956 and in January 1957, he returned with his family to his home in Cuba amidst much sadness from his congregation, which had much affection for the pastor and his family. Agüero had been my pastor for two years and I had collaborated intensely with him in Christian preaching and education. We had formed a deep friendship and I was a witness of how agonising it was for him and his wife to be treated as mere employees and threatened by the Mission. At the conclusion of my university studies, I had decided to enter the Christian ministry and stated my interest to study a Christian education programme, which I found interesting at the Baptist Theological Seminary in Cuba where Agüero had studied. The Mission had been supporting students at the Buenos Aires Baptist Seminary but refused to provide any help for my studies in Cuba and none of the missionaries provided any explanation for this denial.

The crisis also affected those Peruvian Baptists who had left the country for their theological and ministerial formation. In 1955, Julio Villar travelled to Buenos Aires to study at the International Baptist Theological Seminary. In February 1956, three young Peruvians, Fernando Cárdenas, Herbert García and Jacob Padilla, travelled together to Buenos Aires to study at the Seminary. The Mission had promised to pay for their travel and to support them during their studies, aiding them to return to Peru in the summer to carry out ministerial practice in Peruvian churches. The first year continued as planned and in 1957, Jacob Padilla married and returned to the Seminary with his wife, Ruth Escobar. However, Pastor Herbert García records in his autobiographical notes, 'Before I was able to conclude the first semester of my second year (1957), I was surprised, along with my Peruvian colleagues, to no longer receive economic support from the Mission due to the conflict between pastors and missionaries in Peru.'[12] The only ones who continued to receive support from the Mission were Jacob Padilla and his wife. There was never any explanation for the Mission's decision but apparently, the Mission suspected that the students in Argentina had taken sides with Gamarra. Consequently, the students had to depend on the compassion and generosity of Argentinian churches and individuals.

In conversation with some of these brothers from the first generation of Peruvian pastors, they emphasise the importance of the opportunity of being co-pastors alongside active pastors and missionaries on return from their studies. The task of being part of a team and having fellowship and friendship with ministerial colleagues undoubtedly had an important role to play in their formation, a type of aptitude which cannot be learnt through books but only in practice.

Seeds of a Reconstruction

Bryan and Vickey Brasington arrived in Peru in December 1956, and Lowell Ledford arrived in March 1957 to become pastor of the Ebenezer Baptist Church of Miraflores with his wife Shirley. Charles and Martha Bryan arrived in May 1957 and became members of the First Baptist Church in July. Soon after, in September, Bryan became pastor of the church. The spiritual quality and pastoral gifts of Ledford and Bryan were soon evident in their efforts to try and lead these churches towards a conciliatory spirit, seeking to overcome the confrontations of the critical months. Bryan led the First Church in their decision to start meeting again at Wilson Avenue and thus leave the Paseo Colón property in October 1957. The Mission set up its office in this property to guarantee their right to possess and use it.

Charles Bryan was able to effectively lead a process of healing the wounds and returning to fraternal fellowship at the First Baptist Church. Bryan wrote in a report from 31st July 1958, 'There is now a new purified First Baptist Church at a new location and united with the Mission in spirit and purpose.' I, personally, benefited from Lowell Ledford's patient, unflappable pastoral ministry. At the start of 1957, I was teaching at Nuestra Señora de Guadalupe and San Andrés

---

[12] Herbert García, op. cit., 9.

schools, and at the Brown Academy in downtown Lima. This allowed me to get engaged to Lilly Artola, who I had met at the church and who would be my lifelong companion. We were married on 1st March 1958 with Lowell Ledford, our good friend and pastor, blessing the union.

The Mission had set the objective to provide initial theological training to pastors in Peru itself; Sledge developed and took forward the project for a Baptist Theological Institute. Eventually, the Institute was opened on 7th April 1959, initially at the 209 Paseo Colón property where the Mission offices were located. The property was used to provide accommodation for students, as well as classes. Of the nine students the Institute started with, five were from the Ebenezer Baptist Church of Miraflores.

My Ministerial Journey Through the World

By the end of 1958, the International Fellowship of Evangelical Students invited me to become an itinerant supervisor to the different student Bible study groups which were emerging in various Latin American countries. My role was to get to know evangelical university students, encourage them to form Bible study groups in their universities, contribute to their biblical and evangelistic formation while also, whenever possible, carrying out public exposition of the Gospel in universities. I accepted this role and started to work in Peru, Ecuador and Colombia.

For twenty years I worked in student ministries. I am grateful to God for three things that I learnt during these years. Firstly, how to carry out a leadership role without reverting to the egocentric personalism typical of Peruvian autocrats. Secondly, how to study the Bible with a continuously renewed passion for the Word of God, and able to feel the Word as something sweeter than honey, as the Psalmist affirms. Thirdly, for contact with the good evangelical scholarship which started to flourish in the 1960s: F.F. Bruce, John Stott, Bernard Ramm, James Packer and those who subsequently emerged in the Inter-Varsity movement. These three presents I received from the Lord are things which I have always sought to communicate in my ministry.

In 1959, the Fellowship invited me to move to Argentina to collaborate with *Certeza* magazine and Certeza Editions, geared towards readers at university level. I travelled with my wife Lilly to the city of Córdoba in January 1960. In this city, we became members of the Bajo Alberti Baptist Church pastored by Jacob Vartanián, whom I had met at the Baptist World Congress in Rio de Janeiro in 1953. We participated in the life of the church in many ways. Lilly and I also were blessed by the strength and beauty of Christian fellowship, especially when our first son died at ten months old in January 1962.

Working at Certeza Editions was a lesson in literary production under the direction of Alejandro Clifford, a respected preacher, teacher, counsellor and writer. Through him, I became connected with the Plymouth Brethren Churches which were part of one of the historical denominations which had experienced the most growth in Argentina in the early 20th century. The Brethren share the same basic doctrines of faith with the Baptists. The main difference is that in their churches, the ministry is not in the hands of a group of pastors but undertaken by a group of well-prepared lay leaders. In these churches, I also had an intense teaching ministry and learnt much from their dedication and devotion to Scripture.

Dr Arnoldo Canclini, on behalf of the Baptist Publications Board of Buenos Aires, entrusted me to write what would become my first book, *Del Hampa al Púlpito* (Buenos Aires: Junta Bautista de Publicaciones, 1961), to mark the visit of Billy Graham to Argentina late in 1962. It was a story based on the life of a North American youth, Jim Vaus, the son of a minister who lost his way in life and became connected with gangsters in California. During Graham's large-scale evangelistic campaign in Los Angeles (1949), Jim Vaus returned to a living faith in Jesus Christ, his life was transformed and later he started a ministry among youths in a poor neighbourhood of New York. My account was well received and has had five reprints, more than any of my other books.

After Argentina, the student ministry took us to Brazil (1963–1964), then came Spain for doctoral studies (1966–1967), Canada (1972–1975) and back to Peru (1979–1985). In each of these countries, our family joined a Baptist church and we collaborated in many ways with the denomination. As I studied Baptist theology and ecclesiology, I discovered the 16th century Anabaptist roots of our denomination. I realised that these Anabaptist roots could provide a better guidance towards developing a foundation for our social and political responsibility in Latin America. I started to summarise my thinking in my presentation on The Social Responsibility of the Church at the First Latin American Congress on Evangelisation (CLADE IN, Bogota, 1969). The enthusiasm with which the 900 delegates from all over Latin America received my presentation showed me that our evangelical leaders, including Baptists, felt the urgent need for answers to the new questions emerging from the transformation experienced in our societies. This congress was the starting point for the formation of the Latin American Theological Fraternity in Cochabamba, Bolivia in December 1970.

Between 1972 and 1975, my family and I went to live in Toronto, Canada where I was General Director of the InterVarsity Christian Fellowship and as a family we became members of the Spring Garden Baptist Church. For our family, these were years of learning a new language and how to live in a different culture, but I continued to be linked with theological labour in Latin America. In 1972, the FTL celebrated its second congress in Lima on the theme of The Kingdom of God and Latin America. The papers were collected and edited by my colleague, the Baptist Pastor René Padilla from Buenos Aires, and the Baptist Publication House published them as a book in 1975. My paper in this book is called 'The Kingdom of God, Eschatology and Social Ethics and Politics in Latin America'.[13]

Our family, including our two teenage children, Lilly Ester and Alejandro, returned to live in Peru in 1979. That year, the Ebenezer Church of Miraflores ordained me as a pastor and I became a member of the pastoral team alongside a missionary, Esteban Dittmore, and Pastor Herbert García. Our wives, Shirley, Elena and Lilly, were also diligent and effective participants in this team. The church increased its membership and attendance at services almost doubled in the four years we served there. These years of being part of a pastoral team were a challenge in nurturing the essential fraternal relationship needed to preach, teach, pastor and exercise the discipline necessary in aspects of church life.

CONEP asked me, while in Lima, to write a 50-page mimeographed paper providing an evangelical perspective on the liberation theologies which were being spread from Peru. I gathered together materials presented at churches, seminaries and courses for university students. After seeing this work, José Luis Martínez of the Baptist Publishing House from El Paso, Texas, asked me to expand it into a book and it became *La Fe Evangélica y Las Teologías de la Liberación*, a 224-page book (Casa Bautista de Publicaciones, 1987). At the same time, I published in Lima a series of essays which summarised my theological reflection in the previous decade. The Baptist Publishing House decided to publish an edition for all of Latin America with the title *Evangelio y Realidad Social* (revised edition, Casa Bautista de Publicaciones, 1988). I am grateful to the Baptist Publishing House (now Mundo Hispano) who have continued to publish the fruits of my theological research and reflection. The most recent book of mine that they have published is *La Palabra: Vida de la Iglesia,* which consists of twelve biblical reflections on Christian ministry (Mundo Hispano, 2006).

In 1985, the Eastern Baptist Seminary in Wynnewood, Pennsylvania invited me to take over their Missiology Chair. I accepted based on the condition that I would be able to maintain my link with churches, seminaries and theological reflection in Latin America which the seminary, with a strong missionary vocation, accepted. Twenty years of teaching until my retirement in 2005 allowed me to deepen my understanding of the history of Christian mission and the current challenges mission work faces. I had the privilege of finding out more about the Baptist churches of the American Baptist Convention in north United States, which were different in many ways from the Southern Baptists. I have learnt much about their theological position, their missionary vision and their different approach to native believers. From 1997, the Convention's

---

[13] C. René Padilla, Ed., *El Reino de Dios y América Latina* (El Paso: Casa Bautista de Publicaciones, 1975).

International Missions Board and the seminary cooperated sending me as a missionary for six months, first to Peru and then Spain.

In 2001, the Spanish Evangelical Baptist Union (UEBE) requested a lecturer for its seminary, known as the UEBE Protestant Theological Faculty in Alcobendas, near Madrid. My wife and I decided to go to live in Valencia, near our daughter Lilly Ester. In this city, we have been active members since 2001 of the First Evangelical Church of Valencia, on Quart Street. My wife went to be with the Lord in February 2015. I was commissioned for teaching ministry in Spain and while officially retired, I continue collaborating by teaching at Alcobendas and am grateful to God for this privilege. In our church, alongside Pastor Eduardo Delás, we have a plan for systematic preaching of the Bible. As a result, we have published three books; one of those is published by Puma Editions in Peru.[14]

The fruit of my teaching has been summarised in two books: *Tiempo de Misión* (Colombia: Ediciones Semilla-Clara, 1999) and *Como Comprender la Misión* (Buenos Aires: Certeza Unida, 2007). Meanwhile, my work in the last twenty years exploring the person of Christ in Latin American culture is summarised in my two most recent books: *En Busca de Cristo en América Latina* (Buenos Aires: Kairós, 2012) and *Imágenes de Cristo en el Perú* (Sociedad Bíblica Peruana, 2013). I wrote this last book to contribute to the celebration of the 50th anniversary of the Association of Peruvian Evangelical University Groups (AGEUP).

Recovering the Memory

Peruvian Baptists have a task which cannot be put off, which is to recover the historical memory of our churches. There are two works which can aid in this process, two theses dedicated to Baptist history in Peru. The first, written in 1980 by Rosario Vásquez, is based on personal interviews with some of the actors, missionary memoirs and documents published in the denominational magazine, *Destellos Bautistas*. It is the first work worthy of a mention but its own author recognises its limitations and the tentative nature of some of its conclusions. In my opinion, the main limitation of this work is complete dependence on the opinions of just one missionary, Vickey Brasington, to describe the tensions and divisions which occurred in 1956–1958 as she provided a very partial account of the events from the perspective of the second generation of missionaries.

The second work is a master thesis by Gary Crowell, a Southern Baptist missionary, submitted in 1996 at Southwestern Baptist Theological Seminary,

---

[14] Eduardo Delás and Samuel Escobar, *Santiago: la fe viva que impulsa a la misión* (Lima: Ediciones Puma, 2012).

Texas.[15] Crowell had access to the archives of the Southern Baptist Missionary Board which include personal correspondence and official mission reports. He also carried out interviews with some missionaries and Peruvian pastors. Access to mission archives allowed Crowell to provide exact dates and information concerning when missionaries arrived and where they worked. The thesis allows one to understand how certain events unfolded, such as the planting of new churches, and includes a list of missionaries and some statistics on the growth of the work. *This carefully researched and well-organised work offers the missionary's perspective with very little concern for the perspective of Peruvian actors. Historiography will remain unilateral if facts are recorded and interpreted solely from the perspective of missionary writings. Thus, it is significant that the perception of Peruvian believers remains excluded.* In the third edition of Juan Kessler's *Historia de la Evangelización En el Perú*, there are four pages dedicated to Baptists which contain only the most basic information.[16]

The *Destellos Bautistas* magazine is also a useful and valuable source of information. Edited by Vickey Brasington with the assistance of Baptist Theological Institute students, its initial edition published in 1959 was twelve pages long and shaped as a tabloid. The magazine reported on many activities carried out by churches and denominational organisations which appeared in subsequent years.

Two Baptist associations belonging to the CEBP have also attempted to recover this historical memory. In 2009, the La Libertad Association of Evangelical Baptist Churches (ASIEBALL) published a tract, *Baptist History and Principles: Outstanding Events*, by Segundo Rosario Vásquez, Julio Montalvo and Clemente Ávalos. It includes a summary of Baptist history based on the classic by Justo Anderson and a summary of Southern Baptist work in Peru. In 2015, the Lima and Callao Evangelical Baptist Association (ASIEBALC) published a leaflet: *Conociendo los inicios de nuestra obra Bautista,* by Ramón Correa, Segundo Rosario Vázquez and Lucrecia Carrasco. This work is organised pedagogically in four classes containing historical and biblical-theological sections.

What is still missing is an exhaustive historical study which can complement and, at times, correct the limitations of these studies. To move beyond edifying memories and narratives, genuine history requires listening to the voices of different participants, those whose position is closer to the historian's and those which are more distant, including Catholic and secular sources which provide an outsider's perspective. This data then needs to be interpreted with a theological

---

[15] G. Crowell, *op. cit.*
[16] Juan B. A. Kessler, *Historia de la evangelización en el Perú* (Lima: Ediciones Puma, 2010), 247-250.

and missiological focus to discern successes and errors, allowing lessons from the past to contribute to the future. Gary Crowell's work has used much material written by missionaries. What is now missing is the initial labour of collecting national primary sources, such as the minutes of church meetings, correspondence by pastors and national leaders, and oral interviews with actors from different cities and regions.

For example, it is important to hear from different participants to understand the conflicts, initially between Antonio Gamarra and the Mission, and which subsequently involved Luis Manuel Agüero and Alejandro Tuesta. The period between 1955 and 1958 was one of turbulence with regards to different attitudes towards missionary practice and ecclesiastical polity, and few of those who lived through those dramatic moments remain in the First Baptist Church of Lima. Pastor Carlos García and I lived through this period, observing from the Ebenezer Baptist Church in Miraflores and have a Peruvian perspective discerning correct and poor reasons on both sides. The advice offered by the Mission's lawyer, Ribeyro, lacked theological, ecclesiological and pastoral criteria. This part of Baptist history still requires investigating and writing up.

PART TWO

Baptists: Mission and Theology

2: BAPTISTS AND CHRISTIAN MISSION

Estimates indicate that in 1960 there were 36 million Baptists in the world and that by 1995, this number had reached 60 million. This growth of 1.6% a year between 1960 and 1995 is slightly higher than the growth of Christianity as a whole, which was of 1.4% a year, but is lower than that of Pentecostal churches which grew at a rate of 5.2% a year.[1] A scholarly estimate in 1998 suggested that if Baptists maintained their rate of growth, they would have reached 80 million by 2010. Nonetheless, numbers from the Baptist World Alliance suggest that there were 175 million Baptists by 2015.[2] As can be seen, this growth was greater than expected and is undoubtedly due to the vigorous evangelistic activity by growing churches, especially in African, Asian and Latin American countries. These churches are a result of missionaries sent from Great Britain from the 18th century onwards, and from other European countries, as well as the United States and Canada from the 19th century onwards. This understanding of mission as evangelisation has been part of Baptist identity since the 17th century.

In this chapter, I wish to explore some of the most salient aspects of Baptist participation in global Christian mission. We are helped by the fact that the greatest historian of Christian missions is the Baptist Kenneth Scott Latourette (1884–1968), professor of Missions and Oriental History at Yale University, known for his classic seven volume work on the history of the expansion of Christianity.[3] I have chosen not to offer a complete historical survey but present a brief outline that selects certain moments, personae and places which allow us to understand Baptist missionary practice.

For many, the idea of *Christian mission* evokes the image of a geographical movement of specialised personnel dedicated to take the Gospel from Christian

---

[1] These numbers come from Peter Brierley, *Future Church* (Monarch Books, 1998), 141. Brierley uses statistics coming from different databases belonging to specialist organisations such as Mission Advance Research and Communications Centre in Monrovia, California and Global Mapping International of Colorado Springs, United States of America.

[2] Numbers published by the Baptist World Alliance https:/www.bwanet.org.

[3] Kenneth Scott Latourette, *A History of the Expansion of Christianity*, Vol 1-7 (Grand Rapids: Zondervan, 1970).

countries to non-Christian lands. This vision goes hand-in-hand with the concept of territorial churches typical of Christendom, in which those who are born in a Christian country and baptised as children, out of obligation due to social pressure or tradition, are already considered Christians. Baptists have, as a matter of principle, criticised the concept of Christian nations and these days, this concept is regarded as unacceptable even in Europe or the United States. Already in 1928, at the meeting of the International Mission Council in Jerusalem, some missionaries and theologians were warning that European countries required evangelisation as they were losing their Christian identity. The concept of mission as a geographical movement has been replaced by a more biblical concept which affirms the need for the church to be missionary in nature, wherever it is, in its own context or distant lands. A church is not missionary simply because it sends missionaries to distant lands, as if its mission was already fulfilled in its own context. The church is always to have a missionary attitude as all the world is a mission field for God's people.[4]

Those of us who are mission scholars define mission in a wide sense, based on passages such as the synthesis Luke offers us in Acts 2:43–47 and the Apostle Paul's practice. The term *mission* is related to the presence and witness of the church in a society, how the church is a *community* whose members incarnate a lifestyle following the example of Jesus Christ, *the service and prayer* with which this community publicly worships God, the service to human needs which this community carries out, *the preaching* of the Gospel of Jesus Christ as a message of salvation and the *prophetic function* of confronting the evil forces which destroy people and societies.

Nonetheless, the specific concept of *mission* we wish to explore now is related more precisely with the impulse of the Christian church to take the message of Jesus Christ to the four corners of the globe, as the Gospel is for all human beings. When the church is fully conscious that it has been formed and sent to the world with a purpose, it is impelled to fulfil its mission. It is therefore significant that the word *mission* comes from the Latin root *mittere,* which means to send. The historian Justo L. González, expresses this eloquently:

The history of the church is the history of its mission. This is because the church is its mission. The church is born, not when the Lord calls some fishermen, but when he calls them to turn them into fishers of men (Matthew 4:18–22, Luke 5:1–11); not when a group of Christians shut themselves in a room out of fear of the Jews but when Jesus Christ says to these Christians, 'As the Father has sent me, I send you' (Joh 20:19–23); not when the disciples have the mystical experience of seeing

---

[4] I discuss this in more detail in the first chapter of my book, *Cómo comprender la misión* (Barcelona: Editorial Andamio, 2008).

tongues of fire above their heads, but when this experience translates itself into a testimony which overcomes all language barriers (Acts 2:1–11).[5]

Baptist Ecclesiology and Mission

The principles of believer's baptism and the church as a voluntary association of disciples are fundamental in the Baptist experience. These principles lead to the development of an ecclesiology, which logically results in a missionary vocation noticeable from the movement's outset and which explains its significant growth in recent years, and the special moments in its history. These principles are clearly related to the Anabaptist experience of the 16th century on the European continent of communities that had to live their faith and follow Jesus in a world of persecution and marginalisation due to the radical nature of their faith. The Constantinian experience was characterised by the alliance between church and political power, and the exercise of violence with religious goals. Neither Luther nor Calvin questioned this fundamental identification between the religious and political orders. They merely proposed a profound reform of the existing church, while the Anabaptists queried this specific point; for them, all the world, including Catholics and Protestants, princes and paupers equally, were pagans. Their project was not simply the reformation of existing churches but the restoration of the primitive Christian community of true believers.[6] For this reason, in the tempestuous religious atmosphere of the 16th century Catholics, Lutherans, Anglicans and Calvinists rejected the Anabaptists. By rejecting the union between the political order, the church and the practices of this order, such as infant baptism, the Anabaptists decided on a lifestyle open to suffering. In deciding to follow Jesus, they re-discovered the validity of the New Testament model of discipleship in a Christian experience based on a decision and option for Jesus, rejecting the vision and values of the surrounding society.

Baptists: A Unified and Diverse Reality

As the church advances in its proclamation of the gospel, it transforms itself as it extends into different cultures and moments. In this way, the church understands, in a richer way, God's purpose in history so that a church emerges, which is both one and diverse. The missionary process does not follow a single direction from a central place to the periphery. Rather it is multidirectional as the new churches which emerge, which are not simply identical copies of the sending churches, enrich the global picture of a church which is one and diverse. We

---

[5] Justo L. Gonzáles, *Historia de las Misiones* (Buenos Aires: La Aurora, 1970), 23.
[6] Missiologist David J. Bosch explains this phase in *Transforming Mission. Paradigm Shifts in Theology of Mission* (Maryknoll: Orbis Books, 1991).

recognise today that we have to live in the reality of economic and cultural globalisation and thus take into account the reality of a global church when we engage in Christian mission. When we think of the Christian church in the 21st century, we think of a global reality spread across the globe. The words of Jesus have been translated into more than 2,650 languages and continue to be translated. In so many languages, praises are offered to Jesus as Saviour and Lord.

The missionary activity of Baptist churches reflects this wider picture, as the contemporary Baptist reality is both single and multiple. On the one hand, certain distinctive marks of Baptist identity have been maintained, such as personal conversion, believer's baptism, congregational government, the separation between the church and the State, the universal priesthood of believers and the authority of the Bible in matters of faith and conduct. On the other hand, how these principles are applied to different cultural and geographical realities leads to a multi-faceted global reality. Thus, for example, the structure of a church service in an African Baptist church is very different to that of its counterparts in Romania, England, India, Bolivia or Nicaragua. The same can be said about music, acceptable customs regarding eating and drinking and even how church meetings are conducted in these different places. The global Baptist reality is both one and diverse at the same time.

Mobility and Missionary Advance

It should not be forgotten that the first Baptist church, recognised as such, was a church of exiles who had fled religious persecution in England to seek liberty in Holland. Thus, the first two centuries of Baptist denominational history in the English-speaking world provide us with many examples of communities which have moved in search of religious and economic freedom, resulting in the emergence of new churches in new places. This occurred, for example, in British expansion towards the Americas, the Caribbean and Oceania. For example, Baptists arrived in Australia in 1831 and in New Zealand in 1851. By the end of the century, missionaries were leaving these colonies to other parts of the world. This is what we can call the Antioch model. The Antioch Church in Acts of the Apostles was established by Christians fleeing persecution in Jerusalem, who evangelised Jews and Gentiles. Later, this was the first church to intentionally send missionaries on evangelistic trips (Acts 11:19–24 and 13:1–3). Mobility motivated either by economic necessity or religious fervour was decisive in the fundamental role carried out by Baptists in 19th century religious life in the United States. These days, in Europe and the United States, African, Asian and Latin American migrants consider their lives to have a missionary purpose and take advantage of their presence in foreign lands to evangelise and cooperate in churches, even though they have not been officially commissioned as missionaries.

The Baptist Model of Mission

Until the emergence of the great Baptist missionary figures of the Englishman, William Carey (1761–1834) and the American, Adoniram Judson (1788–1850), Christian missionaries had followed the medieval model of mission. In the medieval missionary paradigm, military conquests accompanied evangelisation and monastic orders were responsible for carrying out the missionary task. This is how Catholic missions were carried out in the Americas, Philippines, China and Japan in the 16th and 17th centuries by orders such as Franciscans, Augustinians, Jesuits, Mercedarians and Dominicans, whose rules included vows of poverty, celibacy and discipline. They can be described as elite forces with an iron-clad discipline which allowed them to face the hardship of travelling to unknown lands and learning new languages. They accompanied the process of military conquest and on occasion opposed abuses, such as Bartholomé de las Casas in Spanish America. Even these days the bulk of Catholic missionary work is carried out by monastic orders.

Carey and Judson worked in India and Burma respectively, and were sent as missionaries, with their families, by mission societies and supported by voluntary offerings from ordinary church members. The medieval feudal Catholic mission paradigm was substituted by the modern Protestant paradigm. This is characterised by individualism, faith in reason, the importance of written texts, emphasis on popular education, the rationalisation of social life, the capitalist market and production system, and democratic ideals. What we might call the Baptist missionary paradigm illustrates the Protestant model of mission as described by the historian, Stephen Neill,[7] who reminds us that from their origins in the Moravians of Central Europe, Protestant missions followed a model characterised by five distinctive principles:

- Firstly, *church and school go together* for it is necessary to send children to school if Christians are to be able to read the Word of God.
- Secondly, if Christians are to read the Word of God, *the Bible should be made available in their own language.*
- Thirdly, the preaching of the Gospel needs to be based on a *precise knowledge of a person's mindset.*
- Fourthly, the goal of mission should be a *clear, personal conversion.*
- Fifthly, as soon as possible, there should be an *indigenous church with national leaders.*

---

[7] *A History of Christian Missions* (London: Penguin Books, 1964), 229-231.

William Carey's Missionary Practice

We will pause to investigate William Carey's model of missionary practice. While 1992 was notorious for the celebrations of 500 years of Christopher Columbus' arrival in the Americas, which marked the beginning of Catholic missions in the so-called New World, it was also the 200-year anniversary of the beginning of Protestant missionary work. The reference point for this celebration was the start of William Carey's mission work in 1792 even though, in reality, the Moravian Brethren from Central Europe had been sending missionaries throughout the 18th century and are recognised as the pioneers of Protestant missions. Catholic missions were shaped by the fact that it was the kings of Portugal and Spain who sent the missionaries, and thus Iberian imperialistic expansion went hand-in-hand with the labour of evangelisation. In its extreme form, it followed a philosophy developed in mediaeval Christendom which united military and spiritual conquest summarised by a Catholic historian in the phrase "to conquer first and then to convince".[8]

Three centuries later, Carey's work was the voluntary effort of minority churches, without imperial support, seeking to announce the Gospel to convince people to respond freely to the call to conversion. In this sense, it faithfully reflected profound Baptist missionary convictions. In 1792, William Carey did three things which would become decisive steps for missions in the modern world. First, on 12th May, he published a book which would influence thousands of people. Subsequently, on 31st May, he preached a famous sermon which would have widespread impact. Finally, as a result of this sermon and Carey's tireless labour, on 2nd October a mission society was organised. This would become a model and inspiration for many missionary societies until today. Mission historians affirm that these three events had a decisive influence, leading the English-speaking world to have a large-scale participation in the missionary enterprise.[9]

The title of Carey's book has no less than forty-two words, which clearly summarise the work's content: 'An Enquiry into the Obligations of Christians, to Use Means for the Conversion of the Heathens, in which the Religious State of Different Nations of the World, the Success of Former Undertakings and the

---

[8] Leandro Torres, *Historia de la iglesia en América Latina, 1. La Evangelización* OCHSA, Feres-Friburgo, 1962. A comprehensive study of this conquest missiology and resulting controversies is present in the book by the Peruvian Catholic theologian Gustavo Gutiérrez, *Las Casas in Search of the Poor of Jesus Christ* (Maryknoll: Orbis, 1993).
[9] About Carey one can read Justo L. González and Carlos F. Cardoza, *Historia general de las misiones,* (Barcelona: CLIE, 2008), 146-154; Kenneth Scott Latourette, *A History of the Expansion of Christianity*, Vol 6, *The Great Century: North Africa and Asia* (Grand Rapids: Zondervan, 1976), 104-108.

Predictability of Further Undertakings, are Considered'. Despite not having a university education, Carey had been a tireless reader and student from childhood and this book summarised, in statistical tables and careful descriptions, his perspective on the religious situation across the world at that moment in time. Nonetheless, the book sought not only to inform but also to challenge Christians and convince them that God's word affirmed a missionary demand for all generations and all Christians. The book provided an overview of all the great missionary moments of previous centuries and finally offered practical suggestions concerning how churches could organise themselves to obey their Lord.

Carey preached his famous sermon in May 1792 in Nottingham during the meetings of the Northampton Baptist Association. He based the sermon on a prophecy of Isaiah, which is an invitation to rejoice in the restoration which God works for his people. The passage invites us to widen our perspective concerning what God will do through these restored people. "Enlarge the place of your tent, stretch your tent curtains wide, do not hold back; lengthen your cords, strengthen your stakes. For you will spread out to the right and to the left; your descendants will dispossess nations and settle in their desolate cities (Isaiah 54:2–3). In his sermon, Carey pronounced a phrase which would become famous as the motto of the evangelical missionary movement:

Expect great things from God

Attempt great things for God.

The missionary society, which was founded months later in Kettering, was called The Particular Baptist Society for Propagating the Gospel among the Heathen, which later became known simply as the Baptist Missionary Society. Different from previous evangelical organisations, this organisation shared Carey's vision of taking the gospel to all humanity. This humble shoemaker-preacher and rural teacher had the persistent dream which sought to involve all Christians in an enterprise which would cover all the world. Carey dreamt that his mission society would inspire all Christians of all denominations. This occurred in the following years, in which all kinds of mission societies flourished. Carey also wished to mobilise all Christians and thus any person could become a member of the Missionary Society, contributing large or small amounts of money according to their means.

Carey himself was part of the first contingent of missionaries sent by the Baptist Missionary Society. His experience forms a heart-warming adventure, a feat which illustrates the famous phrase from his sermon. He had the unshakeable faith that God wanted to do great things at that time, and this sustained him in all the adversity he had to face. Yet he also articulated his dreams in major enterprises to which he dedicated himself sacrificially with tireless energy.

Raised an Anglican, a son and grandson of rural teachers, William Carey became a shoemaker's apprentice at the age of fourteen and through his contact with a work colleague, became convinced that personal conversion was necessary to truly be a Christian. As a result of a decisive experience, he became a member of a Baptist church. Before he was twenty, he married Dorothy Plackett who was a faithful companion even though she did not share her husband's missionary vision and enthusiasm. Carey was forced to supplement his meagre stipend as a preacher with work as a shoemaker and rural teacher to survive. He pastored various churches and continued to be a voracious student, especially interested in geography and journeys to distant lands. Books by David Brainerd and John Elliot, who had carried out missionary work amongst native communities in North America, had a great influence on his spiritual progress and the apostle Paul was his favourite hero.

The disquiet which led him to write, preach and organise a missionary society in 1792 led him to offer himself for mission in distant lands. He left for India in 1793 where he worked tirelessly for forty years. He started off as a business manager to support himself while he learnt the Sanskrit and Bengali languages. He faced difficult years of adaptation in Calcutta, which cost the life of his wife, and finally he set up a base in the Danish colony of Serampore to free himself from the opposition of the British colonial authorities. He became a linguist, translator, teacher of native languages and botanist. Nonetheless, he was the strategist of an integral mission which included evangelisation, Bible translation, education, agriculture and medicine.

Carey and his closest companions, Joshua Marshman and William Ward, formed the Serampore Trio. This was a community which shared a home and meals, nurturing a simple lifestyle to carry out the diverse enterprises their missionary purpose demanded. Carey carried out his work without having the privilege of a formal higher education, within the financial restrictions of an enterprise carried out by poor churches trying to continuously establish a strategy for which there was no precedent. His greatest virtue was his firm and persistent patience. Only the divine touch received by someone who expected great things from God can allow us to explain how the life of just one man could be so fruitful in all he attempted for God.

Baptist Advance in North America

It is important to consider the roots of the Baptist presence in North America before exploring the missionary practice of Baptists from the United States. By the time the United States had emancipated itself from British colonial yoke in

1776, Baptists had reached 244 churches and 15,000 baptised members.[10] The influence of Baptist ideas concerning religious freedom can be seen in the way that the constitution of the new republic clearly established the separation between Church and State. The 19th century would be a period of numeric expansion for Baptist churches as part of the westward expansion of the nation. It would also be a time of division among Baptists over issues of race and attitudes towards slavery, as it was in other denominations, such as Methodists and Presbyterians.

In 1814, the nation was still in the armed process of emancipation and faced a blockade by the British Armada; items such as salt and sugar were rare and very expensive. Nonetheless, in this year, Baptists from all over the country met in the city of Philadelphia in May and on 18th December, decided to organise a Baptist convention with the purpose of sending missionaries to the ends of the earth.[11] This is known as the Triennial Convention as it was due to meet every three years and was the first attempt at a Baptist denominational structure in the United States. For historians, the decisive fact is the Baptist decision to organise as a denomination with a missionary purpose as its primary objective.

Year	Number of Churches	Number of members
1814 Triennial	2,470 in 25 states and Canada.	190,351 in USA and Canada
1914 Centenary	53,908 in 48 states and Canada	7,189,155 in USA and Canada
1964 Jubilee	92,657 in USA and Canada	21,958,000 in USA and Canada

The 150th anniversary of the organisation of that first Triennial Baptist Convention of the United States in 1964 allowed a methodical and critical assessment of the noteworthy Baptist advance in that country. Firstly, the statistics concerning the numerical growth of churches and members are impressive and indicate that Baptists have great evangelistic vigour and potential to attract outsiders.[12] For comparative purposes, one can start with 1814, the year of the Convention's organisation; 1914, when it celebrated its centenary and 1964 when it reached its 150-year Jubilee.

---

[10] This statistic refers to 1764 and is present in Davis Collier Wooley, Ed., *Baptist Advance* (Nashville: Broadman Press, 1964), 498.

[11] Ibid., 29.

[12] Ibid., 493.

The 19th century was a century of church growth in the United States, especially for Baptists and Methodists. This growth accompanied two social phenomena: an impressive population growth caused by the considerable arrival of immigrants and the simultaneous expansion of the country towards the West. To have an idea of the importance of immigration, it is sufficient to look at Catholic growth. The North American Catholic Church is fundamentally an immigrant church. A recent document reminds us that in 1790, the Catholic population of 35,000 amounted to only 1.1% of a total US population of 3.2 million. A big increase took place in the 19th century. The number of Catholics increased from 195,000, or 2.5% of the total population, in 1820 to 19.8 million, 18.6% of the total, in 1920."[13] There was a massive influx of Irish immigrants escaping from a famine which ravaged their land and by 2003, Catholics were 23% of the population of the United States.[14] These migratory roots have marked Catholicism in the United States, making it very different from Iberian, Latin American and European Catholicism.[15]

German immigrants were the second most notable group of 19th century arrivals after the Irish and this led to the significant growth of Lutheran churches, especially in the Northeast and the central northern areas of the country. In comparison to Catholicism and Lutheranism, Baptist and Methodist growth was not due to immigration but the direct result of evangelisation. On the one hand, the Methodist revival led to an intensive evangelistic practice which affected other denominations, such as the Baptists. The historian, Mark Noll, affirms that the great beneficiary of the Great Awakening in New England turned out to be the Baptists. In fact, Baptists throughout America – whether in the South, the region surrounding Philadelphia or in New England – embraced evangelical practices and beliefs more rapidly than their counterparts in England."[16] Even today among Baptists in the United States, and especially among Afro-Americans, the word revival means a periodic activity by churches carrying out a special evangelistic effort and a call to renew one's commitment to the Lord. On the other hand, the migratory situation meant that the process of transition opened the minds of many to an active proclamation of the Gospel, as many of them were nominal Christians without a personal faith or active participation in

---

[13] *Zenith* informative bulletin, July 1st, 2006. This bulletin comments on a document produced by Californian bishops in June 2006, "Planning for the Future of California Catholic Church: A Demographic Study".
[14] Bryan T. Froehle and Mary L. Gauthier, *Global Catholicis. Portrait of a World Church* (Maryknoll: Orbis, 2003), 265.
[15] I have discussed this in more detail in my article, "El Catolicismo estadounidense: reflexiones sobre crecimiento número y realidad pastoral", revista *Kairós*, 40 January-June 2007, 109-124.
[16] Mark A. Noll, *The Rise of Evangelicalism* (Downers Grove: Inter-Varsity Press, 2004), 168.

the life of their churches. Thus, some Swedish Lutheran immigrants converted
to Baptist faith and returned to their country with a missionary and evangelistic
vision. Swedish Baptists also pioneered the contemporary evangelisation of
Spain during the 20th century. Baptists and Methodists developed an evangelistic
methodology which was not dependant on religious buildings nor constrained by
institutional bureaucracy. Thus, their preachers could advance on horseback
following the advance of colonists who sought to conquer the West. The custom
of carrying out evangelistic campaigns in large tents emerged in this period and
combined with the aforementioned concept of revival, became a characteristic
of the religious life of many Baptists.

The Afro-American Baptist Churches

It is impossible to acquire a full understanding of North American Baptists if one
does not know the reality of the Black or Afro-American churches. Most Afro-
Americans in the United States are Baptists, and the way Christian mission was
carried out among them during the abominable slavery system is an illustration
of the paradoxes of church history. When we rejoice in the courageous and
effective witness of a figure such as the Baptist pastor Martin Luther King, we
should thank God for the evangelisation of Afro-Americans, even as we
recognise the ambiguities of this evangelistic process.

Latourette offers a brief but detailed overview of this process,[17] first
reminding us that Afro-Americans arrived in the Americas as slaves. It was a
forced rather than voluntary migration which illustrated the terrible ways humans
are capable of treating one another. When one studies with admiration the
histories of ancient Egypt, Greece and Rome, it is important not to forget that
their social systems were based on the existence of a mass of slaves who were
treated as things, not as human beings. With the extension of Christian faith, the
slavery of the Roman world, to which the Bible bears witness, became replaced
by servitude in mediaeval Europe. Nonetheless, Portuguese exploration in
Africa, the Arab slave trade and the need for labour in the Spanish and
Portuguese colonies meant slavery flourished once more in the 16th and 17th
centuries.[18] Africans were victims of a lucrative business which made traders in
Africa, Europe and the Americas wealthy. Slavery occurred in the Portuguese
and Spanish colonial expansion in Iberian America and with British expansion
in the Caribbean and North America, especially in southern colonies where large

---

[17] In chapter 9 of Kenneth Scott Latourette, *A History of the Expansion of Christianity*,
Volume 4, *The Great Century: Europe and the United States* (Grand Rapids:
Zondervan, 1976), 325-366.
[18] *La enciclopedia*, vol. 7 (Madrid: El País, 2003), 5346-5348.

plantations required cheap labour. Slavery would divide Baptists in the United States in the 19th century.

According to estimates, the United States had 757,208 black inhabitants in 1790, approximately 19.3% of the population. In 1910, they were almost ten million but were only 10.7% of the population. Most came from the region surrounding the Gulf of Guinea and were from animistic religions, although there were some Muslims. Nearly all were slaves until 1st January 1863 when President Lincoln abolished slavery. Slaves were dispersed on arrival in American territory, leading to a loss of tribal solidarity, common customs and traditions. Under the absolute dominion of their white owners, they inevitably adopted the customs and lifestyle of their masters and thus, many became Christian through imitation. They started to speak English, albeit with the peculiarities derived from their original languages. Christian inspiration motivated efforts to improve the living conditions of the black population and the effort to abolish slavery. The spiritual revivals which affected the white population led to a movement seeking to evangelise slaves. Emancipation resulted in an increase in efforts regarding evangelism and Christian education.

Currently, the biggest Afro-American Baptist Convention in the United States is the National Baptist Convention which was organised in St Louis, Missouri in August 1886. This convention was preceded by various associations and conventions organised with missionary purposes in the 19th century.[19] Some owners evangelised their slaves and initially black Christians would go to church with their white owners. Later, these black Christians evangelised others and Afro-American churches flourished. Growth among black Christians was greatest in the Methodist and Baptist denominations. There is no agreement about which was the first exclusively Afro-American church although claims are made regarding the antiquity of a church in Savannah, Georgia and another in Silver Bluff, South Carolina, the latter having written evidence that it was established in 1750. Many churches were founded after 1775; the Abyssinian Baptist Church in New York, founded in 1809. is currently the largest.

From the start, Afro-American Baptists have expressed their faith with emotion, enthusiasm and by moving their whole body. These cultural factors have led them to leave, or be expelled, from white churches. These factors also explain the notable growth of these Baptist churches among the black population during the 19th century when Afro-Americans were able to undertake their evangelistic impulse in liberty. These Baptist churches were also the only black collective institutions free from the control of their white owners, where blacks could be themselves in expressing and living their faith. As Latourette indicates, for many years after emancipation the black churches were the main institutions

---

[19] *Baptist Advance*, 190-204.

controlled entirely by blacks. This also accelerated the extension of their faith.[20] Their way of reading and interpreting the Bible from their context of exploitation and their rich musical sensitivity and gifts were expressed in the so-called Negro Spirituals, a genre of sacred music that continues to influence many other cultures. It is no surprise therefore that churches started to carry out a very important role of social integration and transformation, and that Afro-American pastors continue to be both religious and civil leaders who play an important political role.

The 1960s revealed the importance of the deep rootedness of Baptist faith among Afro-Americans and the organisational, educational and missional strength of their churches. At this time, blacks fully engaged with the fight for their civil rights under the leadership of Reverend Martin Luther King (1929–1968) and achieved a noteworthy social transformation through active, non-violent means.[21] When Baptists claim King's fame as a preacher and civil hero, we should not forget his relationship with churches which, along with their enthusiastic singing, also had a practice of serving poor, discriminated people and bravely condemning injustice in public.

Afro-American Baptist churches also maintained a noteworthy interest in global mission. Luther Rice, the tireless promoter of Baptist missions, recognised that Afro-Americans were receptive to the idea of missions and contributed generously. George Lisle (or Liele) was a pioneer in this process. He was born in Virginia in about 1750 and as a slave, accompanied his master, Henry Sharp, to Burke County in Georgia. In time, Sharp recognised Lisle's ministerial talents and excused him from slavery so that he could dedicate himself to preaching the Gospel. Lisle founded the first black Baptist church in Savannah. Later, he travelled to Jamaica and Kingston in 1783, still as a slave but worked and saved to be released in 1784. With other Christians coming from Georgia in 1783, Lisle founded the first black Baptist church on that island. His eloquence as a preacher and the success of his labour led to difficulties with the Anglican Church, the established church in Jamaica; he suffered persecution and was condemned for preaching sedition. Nonetheless, the church continued to grow and in time would be the source of a missionary effort towards Africa.[22] Thus, a black slave was the first Baptist missionary in foreign lands, even before

---

[20] Latourette, *A History of the Expansion of Christianity*, Volume 4, *The Great Century: Europe and the United States*, 327.

[21] The Spanish pastor Emmanuel Buch, one of Martin Luther King's biographers, defines the personality of this notable social leader: pastor, Baptist, black, in *Martin Luther King* 3rd edition (Madrid: Fundación Emmanuel Mounier, 2001).

[22] *Baptist Advance*, 194. Baptist history in Jamaica is briefly described in Horace O. Russell, "La iglesia en el pasado: un estudio sobre los bautistas jamaquinos en los siglos XVIII y XIX" in Jorge Pixley ed., *Hacia una fe evangélica latinoamericana. Una perspectiva bautista* (San José: DEI, 1988).

William Carey. Later, Lott Carey, as member of the First Baptist Church of Richmond, Virginia, was inspired by Rice to organise the Richmond African Baptist Missionary Society in April 1815. In 1819, both Carey and Colin Teague were nominated as missionaries to Africa by the General Baptist Convention and left for Liberia in January 1821.

Civil War and Division among Baptists

Throughout the 19th century, Baptists, along with other denominations in the United States, were confronted by the issue of slavery. From the start of the colonial period, Quakers had freed their slaves and declared themselves against slavery. The great promoter of anti-slavery societies, Benjamin Lundy (1789–1839), was a Quaker. Due to their concern with religious freedom and their refusal to involve themselves in politics, Baptists shied away from the theme of slavery. Nonetheless, the Ketockton Baptist Association of Virginia in 1787 determined that to inherit slaves was to disobey the divine law and formed a commission to present a plan of progressive emancipation.[23] Some local associations and conventions started putting the fight against slavery on their agenda and in Philadelphia in 1789, abolitionist societies were accredited and their promotion in all churches recommended. Nonetheless, some conventions and associations in the South took the decision to not involve themselves in political issues. This was the case, for example, of South Carolina where approximately one third of Baptists and one fifth of pastors were slave-owners.[24]

Social evolution in the north of the United States had made the continuation of slavery unsustainable. The abolitionist movement grew vigorously, which was motivated and sustained by people working from Christian principles concerning the dignity of every human being. The existence of slavery was considered incompatible with the democratic principles and values expressed in the constitution of the United States. The efforts of the abolitionist movement came to fruition when President Lincoln declared the abolition of slavery in 1863. Latourette recognises and explains the direct relationship between spiritual revivals and the increasing awareness that it was impossible to support slavery from the perspective of Christian ethics: not only were the most renowned leaders led to oppose slavery due to their Christian principles but also many less well-known figures were motivated by a desire to act according to Christian principles.[25] He indicates that the anti-slavery movement led to polarisation in the whole country: "the hope that reason and appeals to conscience would lead

---

[23] Torbet, *A History*, 282.

[24] Ibid., 283-284.

[25] Latourette, *A History of the Expansion of Christianity, Volume 4, The Great Century: Europe and the United States*, 350.

slave owners to repent and free their slaves disappeared."[26] The southern states, economically dependent on slave labour, were opposed to the anti-slavery movement which was mainly based in the North. Southern protestant ministers preached in defence of slavery affirming that it was wise, benevolent and biblically-based.[27]

Many denominations with national organisations divided over this issue. The increasing controversy and polarisation led to division specifically because of mission work.[28] The Triennial Baptist Convention, formed in 1814, gathered together the missionary effort of Baptists across the country including both northern and southern states. The key issue concerned whether the mission board could send slave owners as missionaries. In 1840, the American Baptist Convention, which was anti-slavery, met in New York to discuss this issue as some missionaries in Burma had decided to break ties with the Triennial Convention as they did not want to associate with slave-owning missionaries. In November of that same year, the Alabama Baptist Convention decided to withdraw funds from the Foreign Missions Board until it received assurances that it had cut ties with the abolitionist movement. The anti-abolition movement became stronger in the south, leading to the formation of the Southern Baptist Convention as southern Baptists decided to separate from the national Convention. In less than two centuries, Baptists, who had emerged with a Biblical perspective which confronted the social order in the struggle for religious liberty, divided over their complete identification with the existing social order. Latourette's comment has a veiled tone of lament: "The tie of love proved to be too weak to face the tension caused by a love horrified at the spectacle of black servitude. Christianity had proved its impotence to control the forces that had been released."[29]

The division among Baptists affected the two great conventions which emerged from it. Northern Baptists were characterised by social activism and the practice of an integral mission and open theological reflection but, in some sectors, lost their evangelical identity. Possibly for this reason, along with other denominations in the industrial and urban north, it was affected by a numerical decline through the slow loss of members and the absence of a vigorous evangelisation. Their missionary work in other continents has reflected the denomination's deep theology and integral emphasis, leading to a more fraternal and respectful relationship with national Christians. Southern Baptists would be characterised by a strong social conformity to the values of a nationalist, elitist and still racist society. On the other hand, they maintained an intensive

---

[26] Ibid.
[27] Ibid.
[28] Torbet, A History, 287.
[29] Ibid., 351.

evangelisation, not only in the south, but in all the country and thus had significant numerical growth. Its missionary effort in the rest of the world reflected this focus on evangelism and social conformity, becoming characteristics of the churches which emerged from its evangelistic work in other countries.

Baptists from the United States in Global Mission: Adoniram Judson

Adoniram Judson (1788–1850), his wife, Ann Hasseltine (1789–1826) and his missionary colleague, Luther Rice (1783–1836), emerged in the first decades of the 20th century to play the same role among the Baptists of the United States that William Carey and the Serampore Trio carried out for Baptists in Great Britain and the rest of the world. Judson was a brilliant student from a congregational background, able to research various disciplines. During his studies at Andover Seminary in Boston, he went through a spiritual revival. As news about Carey's missionary journey to India started to spread around the United States, many young people were awakened to the missionary cause in Asia. In 1810, Judson and some colleagues informed their church of their desire and intention to go to Asia as missionaries, setting the stage for what would unfold. In response to the enthusiastic request of these young people, the Congregational Church founded the American Board of Commissioners for Foreign Missions (ABCFM) which became the means for sending missionaries and promoting missions.[30] Baptists on the Atlantic, from Charleston to Boston, were already offering and supporting Carey's work in India. Even though this new organisation did not belong to their denomination, Baptists contributed $3,000 to mission work in Asia.[31]

In 1812, under the supervision of the Congregational board, Judson, his wife and Luther Rice embarked on the journey to India where they would meet Carey. During his ship's journey, Judson decided to carry out a detailed study of the theme of baptism in the Bible to refute Carey. Nonetheless, he arrived at the conclusion that the Baptists were correct to consider baptism as a step to be taken after conversion and he begun to question the validity of his infant baptism in the Congregational church so that on arrival in Calcutta, India, Judson, his wife and Luther Rice were baptised by Carey. This led them to resign from the Congregational Board and seek support among Baptists. Due to pressure from the British East India Company, they were forced to leave India in 1813 and went to the city of Rangoon in Burma seeking to start missionary work in that

---

[30] Kenneth Scott Latourette, *A History of the Expansion of Christianity, Vol 4 The Great Century: Europe and the United States*, 80-81.
[31] Torbet, op. cit., 248.

kingdom.[32] At this time, Luther Rice returned to the United States and dedicated himself to promote Baptist support for Judson, for which he found a propitious environment, leading to the formation of the Triennial Baptist Convention in 1814, which we have already mentioned.

Judson and his wife's work in Burma was noteworthy and exemplary, becoming a reference point for the missionary efforts of Baptist missionaries in other parts of the world. They dedicated themselves to evangelisation and Bible translation as their first objective. They also established a school and adopted some orphan girls. By 1824, Judson had completed a dictionary of the Burmese language and moved to the city of Ava to be in better contact with the government to allow them to proceed with their labour. Subsequently, the Anglo-Burmese war began and although he was not British, Judson was treated as a spy and imprisoned for twenty months. He became seriously ill due to fever, malnutrition and a forced march. His wife, Ann, continued bravely and carried out numerous interventions to achieve his freedom, which took place in 1826. Soon after, the Burmese government asked Judson to serve as a translator for the Treaty of Yandabo which brought the war to an end. Ann Judson died in that same year due to complications from contracting variola. Judson moved to Moulmein in 1828, setting up a church and a school.

By 1834, Judson had managed to complete the translation of the whole Bible into the Burmese language and at the end of this year, he married for a second time to Sarah Hall (1803–1845), widow of his missionary colleague, George Dana Boardman (1801–1831). Sarah was a notable linguist and pedagogue who had worked on the translation of the New Testament into the language of the Karen tribe, which had received the Gospel with enthusiasm. After their marriage, she worked intensively alongside Judson, with whom she had eight children. Her health started to deteriorate and in 1845, she died on a journey back to the United States. Judson was also ill; nonetheless, during his nine month stay, he carried out numerous visits to churches and universities where he was warmly received for his work in Burma. While visiting the University of Madison in New York State, he met Emily Chubbuck (1817–1854), whom he married before returning to Burma in 1846. Judson continued to work intensely, despite his poor health, to complete a dictionary of the Burmese language shortly before his death in 1849.

---

[32] Gerald H. Anderson, Ed. *Biographical Dictionary of Christian Missions* (New York: Macmillan Reference, 1998), 345. In this dictionary there are articles about Judson and each one of his successive wives.

Global Impact of Baptist Mission

The Baptist missionary movement in the 19th and 20th centuries followed a model left by the mission work of William Carey and Adoniram Judson, which was very different from that of the mediaeval Catholic model. These principals explain the type of Protestantism to emerge in Asia, Africa, Oceania and Latin America as a result of protestant missionary work in the last few centuries. In Asia and Africa, the arrival of Protestant missionaries in the 19th century coincided with the arrival of the British and other European empires. Many Asians and Africans reflect critically on this alliance between empire and mission. Nonetheless, it is important to point out that mission within a modern paradigm had more opportunities to be a force of social transformation, so that colonised people could achieve their own liberation and fight in favour of a more just social order. Locals learned how to read the Bible in their own language at missionary schools, dignifying their culture. These schools educated the leadership of autochthonous churches where horizontal, non-paternalistic relationships were developed, essential for democracy. These missionary schools also educated the political leaders who would lead their people towards freedom from the European colonial yoke.

The careers of Carey and Judson illustrate another specific characteristic of the Baptist model of mission: the missionary travels overseas with his family and from his home carries out the task of evangelism and service. As has already been mentioned, Catholic monastic orders carried out the medieval mission paradigm in the Americas, Philippines, China and Japan in the 16th and 17th centuries. These missionaries were single due to their vow of chastity. Even now, most of the Catholic missionary labour continues to be done through monastic orders. In contrast, the family life of Carey and Judson illustrates some of the difficulties in the Baptist model of mission in terms of health, cost and the specific difficulties of moving families into a new environment in a foreign land. At the same time, this aspect of the Baptist model reveals the potential for missionaries to model a different form of family life, which would be a visible illustration of the Gospel values they preached.

Women have a fundamental role in the Baptist model of mission. The historian, Dana Robert, emphasises the fact that Judson's second wife, Sarah Hall, was a Bible translator, a role limited to men in other missionary societies. Two of the most notable itinerant evangelists, Deborah Wade and Calista Vinton, also worked in Burma. Baptists were the first mission board to send a single woman as a missionary: in 1815, Charlotte White, a widow, joined Judson's team in Burma.[33] Women had an essential role in creating support structures for

---

[33] Dana L. Robert, *American Women in Mission* (Mercer: University Press, 1996), 53-55.

foreign missions. The Foreign British Bible Society was possibly the first Christian organisation to form voluntary societies to support both the sale of Bibles, and fundraising.[34] Throughout the 19th century, women's' unions emerged in various denominations for this purpose. One of the most important Baptist missionaries was Carlota (Lottie) Moon (1840–1912) who was sent to Shandong in China by the Southern Baptists in 1873. In 1885, she moved to the Pingdu province where she worked alone as an evangelist and preacher.

Although in the south there was opposition to women pastoring or teaching men, Carlota continued to report her activities, challenging men to join the missionary labour in China. She postponed her time of rest in the United States due to the receptivity of the Gospel in China and in 1887, she wrote a letter asking Southern Baptist women to organise themselves to raise funds to support more missionaries. This led to the formation of the Auxiliary Woman's Missionary Union which would play a fundamental role in Southern Baptist missionary work. In countries where they sent missionaries, national churches would set up similar female organisations. Hence, in Latin America and Spain, Baptist womens' organisations are called Woman's Missionary Unions. The most important mission offering in the south of the United States is named after Carlota Moon.

The Baptist conviction that church structure should be neither hierarchical nor bureaucratic allowed Baptist missionaries, when they undertook missionary work in other regions and cultures, to encourage new believers to actively participate in the ongoing evangelistic labour, and in the government of the new churches that were planted. Thus, we encounter indigenous leaders of the receiving countries taking on responsibilities. For example, a young church, such as the Jamaican Baptists, soon organised a mission to other countries, especially in Africa. The same occurred amongst the Karen in Myanmar and Baptists in Argentina, Brazil and India. In a biographical dictionary of Christian mission among approximately a dozen Baptist missionaries from Europe and the United States, we can also find examples of indigenous missionaries from the countries mentioned above.[35]

Ko Tha Byu (1778–1840), from the Karen tribe in Burma, underwent a spectacular conversion and was baptised in 1828. He worked for twelve years among his people, becoming known as the Karen apostle as his preaching was received by thousands in his tribe; currently, the Karen Baptists account for half of Burmese Christians.[36] Krishna Pal (c. 1764–1822) was the first Indian baptised at the Serampore Mission in Bengal in 1800 and was ordained as an associate

---

[34] Andrew F. Walls, *The Cross-Cultural Process in Christian History* (Maryknoll: Orbis, 2002), 233.

[35] These examples are taken from Gerald H. Anderson, op. cit.

[36] Ibid., 373-374.

minister for the English missionaries in 1806. A natural evangelist and a hymn writer, he carried out an itinerant preaching ministry in various regions and eventually among the Khasi tribe.[37] Mamie Johnson (c. 1820–1888), who was born a slave in Jamaica, went to Africa after her freedom to the island of Fernando Po, and then to Douala. Alfred Saker, a Baptist Missionary Society missionary, encouraged Mamie, a teacher and an evangelist, and her husband to open a mission in Douala. There most noteworthy work was to start up protestant work in Cameroon.[38]

Baptists in Latin America

American Baptists (from the north of the United States) and Southern Baptists were responsible for most of the Baptist missionary work in Latin America, although British and later, German Baptists were also interested in sending missionaries to Latin America. Baptist growth was greatest in Brazil, followed by Argentina, Mexico, Puerto Rico, Bolivia and Central America. American Baptists began their work in Latin America through the Domestic Missions Board, while the Southern Baptists worked through the Foreign Mission Board. I have defended elsewhere that although Baptists were not the fastest growing denomination, an Anabaptist disposition characterises all Latin American Protestants. Faced with a decadent Christendom, with the official Catholic Church on the defensive, Protestants emerging from mission work critiqued Catholicism, defending religious freedom and the separation between Church and State. In the first generations, all Protestants practiced a discipleship dedicated to integral mission and willingness for sacrifice and suffering.[39]

The Scottish Baptist, Diego Thompson, arrived in South America during the process of emancipation from Spanish colonial yoke (1810–1824) and, as indicated in this book's first chapter, is considered the precursor of Protestant missionary presence in Latin America. Thompson nurtured friendships with the leaders of the independence movement: the Argentine, José de San Martin, the Chilean, Bernardo O'Higgins in the South, and the Venezuelan, Simón Bolívar in the North. Thompson's initial work led to the first teacher-training schools in Argentina, Chile and Peru. In each country, he managed to cooperate with priests who were interested in the Bible, some of whom would continue his educational

---

[37] Ibid., 512.
[38] Ibid., 336-337.
[39] I have defended this visión briefly in "El reino de Dios, la escatología y la ética social y política en América Latina" in C. René Padilla Ed., *El Reino de Dios y América Latina* (Santo Domingo: Casa Bautista de Publicaciones, 1975), 127-156.

work and Bible promotion.[40] It was in the latter part of the 19th century that missionaries arrived with the specific purpose of planting churches. We will focus on four countries where Baptists arrived through different means and thus illustrate the different aspects of Baptist missiology: Brazil, Argentina, Bolivia and Nicaragua.

In the case of Brazil, Baptists who had migrated from the south of the United States during the American Civil War asked Southern Baptists, in 1871, to send missionaries and pastors to meet their spiritual needs and evangelise the country. The Baptist pioneers, the Bagby family, arrived in Brazil in 1881 and the Taylor family joined them the following year. A Brazilian priest, Antônio Teixeira de Albuquerque, converted to Protestantism through his own study of the Bible and having reached Baptist convictions, he joined the Bagbys and the Taylors as they carried out an intensive evangelisation labour in Salvador, Bahia. From Salvador, churches expanded to the capital, Rio de Janeiro, to the north in Belem, and later the whole country. From 1892 onwards, Baptists came from Germany, Hungary, Lithuania and Bulgaria as part of an intensive migratory movement. These migrants set up churches which cooperated with the new Brazilian churches, leading to the formation of regional associations, the first being in Recife in 1901. The *Jornal Batista* newspaper was established that same year and would play an important role in education and forming a collective identity.

The Brazilian Baptist Convention was organised on 22nd June 1907 in the city of Salvador with forty-three delegates from thirty-nine Baptist churches. Significantly, the Foreign Missions Board was organised at the same time as the convention to respond to a request from Chilean Baptists for assistance. In 1908, Baptist women took the initiative to form the Woman's Missionary Union which carried out an educational role among children and youth concerning overseas missions. The mission board sent Taylor as a missionary to Portugal where initial growth led to the formation of a Portuguese Baptist Convention in 1920. From the outset, the work was characterised by the active participation of Brazilian leadership so that missionaries did not monopolise the initiative. Another important characteristic of Brazilian Baptists is that since this initial stage, Baptists participated in Brazil's political life at local, regional and national level.

Pablo Besson (1848–1932), a Swiss erudite pastor educated in Germany, became convinced of Baptist principles through his New Testament studies and having served as a missionary in France under the Northern Baptist Missionary Society of the United States, became a Baptist pioneer in Argentina. Argentina,

---

[40] For biographies of Thomson see: Arnoldo Canclini, *Diego Thomson, Apóstol de la enseñanza y distribuición de la Biblia en América Latina y España* (Buenos Aires: Sociedad Bíblica Argentina, 1987); and Donald Mitchell, "The Evangelical Contribution of James Thomson to South American Life 1818-1825." Unpublished doctoral dissertation, Princeton Theological Seminary, 1972.

like Brazil, is a country of immigrant colonists and a French-speaking group of evangelicals in the Esperanza colony, in the province of Santa Fe, wrote to Besson asking for a pastor. Not finding a suitable candidate and being single, Besson decided to travel to Argentina himself. As he did not find any missionary agency to support him, he sold his belongings to pay for the fare.

On arrival in 1881, he started his ministry among French immigrants and soon had to face Roman Catholic fanaticism expressed in a monopoly over cemeteries, and a refusal to allow the existence of a civil register for non-Catholic citizens. This led Besson to decide to focus his efforts on the struggle for religious liberty so that without abandoning his role as pastor and evangelist, he also became a political activist and writer in favour of religious liberty. He put his erudition in service of this cause and wrote for all the major newspapers in the country, being respected for the quality of his journalistic work. Eventually, liberal politicians achieved the creation of a civil register. Besson also made his own translation of the New Testament into Spanish, a carefully annotated edition that even today is recognised as valuable.

Argentinian Baptists organised themselves in a convention in 1908 and worked intensively to evangelise the interior of the country. In 1919, they sent Maximino Fernández, Enrique Molinas and Celestino Ermili as missionaries to the neighbouring country of Paraguay, where they carried out an intensive work of evangelisation in the face of Catholic persecution. Later, in cooperation with Northern Irish Baptists, they sent missionaries to the south of Peru.[41]

The South American Andean region, which includes Colombia, Ecuador, Peru and Bolivia, is characterised by the presence of an ultra-conservative Catholicism and a deep-rooted syncretistic indigenous popular religion. Canadian Baptists sent the first missionary to Bolivia, Archibald Brownie Reekie (1862–1942), in 1899. Reekie used his diplomatic talents to avoid conflict with the Catholics and started his work with children and youths who wanted to learn English. This led him to contact liberal politicians who supported the expansion of his educational ministry. However, he did not lose his evangelistic vision and soon congregations began to appear. While missionaries took the initiative in evangelistic work, they were able to progressively hand it over to national leaders, leading to the formation of the Bolivian Baptist Union in 1936. One of the Union's first steps was to seek to evangelise Bolivia's mining centres.

The denomination grew and carried out noteworthy social and educational work. In 1911, the new constitution permitted religious freedom, partly a consequence of literature on religious freedom and direct political intervention. One event had a powerful impact on the country. An evangelical organisation

[41] Rogelio Duarte, *El Desafío protestante en el Paraguay* (Asunción: Centro Cristiano de Comunicación Creativa, 1994), 81ff and Justice Anderson, *An Evangelical Saga* (Maitland: Xulon Press, 2005), 198, 202.

which had an agricultural project among the indigenous people in Huatajata, a rural area on the shores of Lake Titicaca, donated some land to the Baptist mission. Despite their social efforts, there were no conversions and no churches emerged in this region. The missionaries were surprised to discover that along with the lands, they had received some peasant families as property. These families saw themselves as servants of the missionaries and believed they were forced to adopt the Baptist faith, as in the case of their Catholic owners. After a self-critical assessment and strategic plan, the Mission decided to hand over the land with its legal registration to these families in 1942. Soon, churches started to grow as the peasants felt they had chosen their Baptist faith freely. When a revolutionary government carried out land reform in Bolivia in 1952, it referred to the handing over of lands in Huatajata as a precedent for this distributive justice. In 1949, an angry indigenous mob, spurred on by a Catholic priest, attacked a leadership meeting and killed the Canadian Baptist missionary, Norman Dabbs, a pastor, Carlos Menezes, the president of the Baptist Union, Francisco Salazar, and five lay Christians. This tragedy consolidated and strengthened the Baptist work. The Baptist Union grew in cities, mining centres and mountainous rural zones in West Bolivia. In East Bolivia, Brazilian missionaries introduced the Baptist message in 1946 and in 1952, organised the Bolivian Baptist Convention.

The world press paid much attention to Nicaragua in the final decades of the 20th century due to the country's agitated political life in which intervention by the United States has been a decisive factor. The Somoza dictatorship was one of the bloodiest in Central America, followed by a civil war in which the left-wing Sandinista revolutionaries prevailed. The medical doctor, Gustavo Parajón, son of one of the first Baptist pastors, became the most respected Protestant figure during these turbulent years. Parajón was one of the founders of CEPADE, an inter-denominational organisation created to administer the foreign aid coming to the country due to the earthquake which destroyed the nation's capital, Managua, in 1974. This organisation became famous for its efficiency and transparency in administering evangelical aid, a clear contrast to the corruption and inefficiency with which the Samosa government used the vast aid received from across the world to enrich Samosa and his family. Even during the most tense years of the civil war, CEPADE was respected by both sides.[42]

The First Baptist Church had been organised in 1917 when pastors Brewer, Stomp and Brink, from the Domestic Missions Board of the Baptists in the north of the United States, visited a group of dissidents from the Central American Mission which was under the leadership of the British missionary, Eleanor

---

[42] The situation within Nicaragua and the role of Baptists is discussed in Raymond P. Jennings "When President and Missionary Disagree: American Baptists Wrestle with a Basic Question", *American Baptist Quarterly*, December 1984, 306-314.

Blackmore.[43] Brewer baptised thirty people, according to their convictions, including pastor José Mendoza, in Lake Nicaragua and they organised themselves as a church. Evangelisation, accompanied by medical and educational work and with the help of the Northern Baptists, led to a period of growth so that in 1937, the National Baptist Convention of Nicaragua was organised with 2,500 members divided into twenty-one churches. By 2000, the Convention had seventy-nine churches and 10,000 baptised members.

Educational institutions set up by Baptists, such as schools and universities, have served the evangelical community and the general public across Latin America. The Casa Bautista de Publicaciones (Baptist Publishing House), based in El Paso, Texas, has offered an important service to all Protestants, now known as the Editorial Mundo Hispano. It has existed for over a century and has representatives in all Spanish-speaking countries. It was the fruit of the vision of the Southern Baptists and in being handed over to a Latin American Baptist leadership, it no longer limits itself to publishing denominational material and publishes books by a variety of evangelical authors.

Baptist Missiological Foundations

As indicated above, Carey, Judson and other great Baptist mission pioneers reflected Baptist principles concerning a Christian's personal life, as well as the nature and function of the church in their mission work. At the risk of being repetitive, it is important to summarise the main principles of what we could call a Baptist missiology, which form a heritage worthy of consideration when faced with the specific challenges that the missionary context of the 21st century provides.

Mission at one's own door and the other side of the ocean

Carey, Judson and their colleagues in Asia first put their missionary passion into practice in their own countries. Recent research indicates that each member of the Serampore Trio had been active in evangelism, pastoral work and service to the poor in their home environments in England and Scotland. Carey's aforementioned book had paragraphs which expressed his militant attitude against the slave trade and both his companions had been trade unionists, supporting social causes. Thus, the journey to India was not a means of escaping the missionary demands in his own country but a way of fulfilling an evangelistic vocation, an evangelistic zeal for those that Carey called pagans, those in distant lands who had never heard the Gospel but were now accessible through trade and commerce. Nonetheless, the missionary passion of these men had been put

---

[43] Baptist work in Nicaragua is summarized well in Gerald H. Anderson, op. cit., 439-450.

to the test in their own country in an effort which was not always recognised or well-paid. The best mission school for those who go to the other side of the world is authentic mission in their own context.

Mission that seeks personal conversion

Carey had the Baptist and evangelical conviction that at the centre of evangelism lies the call to a personal relationship with Jesus Christ. Likewise, Judson became convinced of his personal salvation and asked to be baptised. They represented a missionary movement connected to the fervour of Central European pietists and Moravians that had emerged as a spiritual revival amid a nominal and cold Protestantism. This deep evangelical conviction is the foundation for the Baptist advance in Asia, Africa, and especially Latin America.

These convictions regarding personal conversion to Jesus are in open contrast with the sacramental concepts and practices of traditional Catholic missiology, and the loss of evangelistic vigour in ecumenical Protestantism. A Catholic historian of Spanish missions in the 16th century has affirmed that "the essential goal of missions among the infidels is not the conversion of individuals but to establish a visible church, with all the organisations and institutions which this implies."[44] This concept is at least partly responsible for the nominalism in a continent which is Christian only in name, even though there is a whole complex and prestigious ecclesiastical apparatus, and religious buildings are everywhere to be seen.

Contextual mission

Carey and Judson worked tirelessly to translate Scriptures into the numerous languages which were spoken in their mission fields. The central importance of having the Scriptures in the local language reflects Baptist convictions regarding the authority of God's Word. Although Catholics had been in India and other countries since the 16th century and had studied native languages, they had not worked on Bible translation. The same happened in Peru. Catholic missionaries translated catechisms into Quechua, but the translation of Holy Scripture only occurred with the arrival of Protestant missionary pioneers. In 1901, the American Bible Society managed to complete a translation of the four gospels, Acts of the Apostles and Romans into Quechua by the great Cuzco novelist, Clorinda Matto de Turner, who was in exile in Argentina.[45]

---

[44] Robert Ricard. *La conquista espiritual de México* (Mexico City: Fondo de Cultura Económica, 1991), 21. I deal with the missiological contrasts between Catholics and Protestants in the fifth chapter of my book, *Tiempo de misión.*
[45] See William Mitchell, *La Biblia en la historia del Perú* (Lima: Sociedad Bíblica Peruana, 2005).

Along with his concern for all of humanity, which we have already mentioned, Carey was convinced that a strong, autochthonous church was only possible with the translation of the Bible into the local language. Thus, Carey's press in Serampore had distributed complete versions and portions of the Bible in forty-five languages and dialects. It also published grammar and dictionaries which would be useful for the whole Indian population.

Carey also sought to provide high quality training and preparation for Indian pastors and evangelists. This preparation consisted not only of Biblical and theological studies, but also a better understanding of India's different religions and philosophies. Carey and his associates translated the famous epic poem, *Ramayana*, into English to encourage a better comprehension of the different dimensions of Indian culture. It is impossible to deny the respect that these missionaries had for these local cultures, even though this required considerable effort. Although critics claimed that such a detailed study of Indian culture was a waste of time, these missionaries were aware that effective preaching of the Gospel demands an understanding of the mind set of the people to whom one is preaching.

Integral mission

Carey ensured that the educational work carried out reached the Indian youth who needed it, even if they were not Christians. Likewise, he nurtured his interest in plants and gardening, becoming an expert in local botany, writing specialised papers and corresponding with experts from all over the world. He organised the Agricultural and Horticultural Society of India, seeking to improve soil usage and increase food production. He introduced European fruit plants and carried out experiments planting coffee, cotton, sugar cane and cereals. In his mission practice, Carey demonstrated that strong evangelical convictions regarding the Gospel and conversion can go hand-in-hand with action in favour of different human needs. Carey, a mission pioneer engaged in a Biblical model of mission, would have considered the debates within some contemporary mission societies concerning the lack of value of social work as meaningless.

New Testament style of mission

Carey and his companions sought an incarnational approach in the country they chose to work in. They often worked sacrificially in their original professions to cover the costs of their mission work. They developed a common fund to become as independent as possible from the mission board in England, to be able to develop a strategy which responded to local needs more than the inadequate perceptions and expectations of a distant entity. Likewise, they sought through this to release funds for work in other parts of the world. They lived together, sharing the same roof and food to save funds, and thus dedicated themselves to their vast literary and educational enterprise. They faced opposition from British colonial authorities who saw their evangelistic work as counter-productive for imperial administration.

Neither Carey, nor Judson, nor their mission work was perfect. Internal difficulties caused by differences in priorities, personality and generational perception magnified the impact of external difficulties. They were not able to fully disassociate themselves from the European imperial presence in India, which often brought more darkness than light. In Carey's case, initial colonial opposition was later replaced by openness to cooperate in educational and cultural tasks. Lack of funds and difficulties in the relationship with the Baptist Missionary Society in England led Carey and the Serampore Trio to seek funds in Bengal and Calcutta. Nonetheless, they still sought to base their presence and methodology on Biblical principles and not on the model provided by the British Empire.[46] This led them to pay the price of misunderstanding and persecution, but observing their heritage 200 years later, there are many reasons to praise God.

Latourette, the great historian of Christian missions who we have already mentioned, makes an important observation concerning Baptist missionary work, that both in their expansion in the United States and in other parts of the world, Baptists have generally worked with the poorest sectors of society while other denominations have dedicated themselves to the governing elites. This can be clearly observed in the case of Afro-American slaves in North America and in the case of ethnic communities in the Asian countries we have mentioned. In his prologue to Robert Torbet's *A History of the Baptists*, Latourette declares, "most Baptists were humble in the eyes of the world and on the whole did not receive a place in human memory. Nonetheless they were great souls and dreamt and built much more than they could imagine. It has been a great privilege granted to the Baptists, more than any other Christian body of similar size, to preach the Gospel to the poor".[47] Even so, Torbet himself states that while Baptists on the whole have not placed their emphasis on a social gospel, "as Baptist ministry has been directed at humble people, precisely those socially, politically and economically disenfranchised, it is perfectly natural that social reforms can be considered among their contributions to Protestantism and life in countries where Baptists have worked".[48]

Since the start of the 20th century, Latin American Baptists have participated in the global missionary enterprise. Thus, for example, Brazil sent missionaries to Angola and Portugal, and Puerto Rico to Central America. In the last decades of the 20th century, Latin American missionary presence in Asia, Africa and Europe, sent and supported by Latin American churches, has increased. As I now

---

[46] For a critical yet appreciative study based on recent research see Christopher Smith, 'A Tale of Many Models: The Missiological Significance of the Serampore Trio' and the response by William O'Brien in *Missiology*, Vol. 20, No. 4, October 1992, 479-507.
[47] Robert G. Torbet, op. cit., 8.
[48] Ibid., 485.

live in Spain, I will conclude on a personal note. In 2014, in Torrox, near Malaga on the south Mediterranean coast of Spain, I was invited to talk to a gathering of Latin American missionaries convened by Dr Samuel Cueva, a Peruvian missionary in London. There were 102 Latin American missionaries present who worked in various European countries and shared their witness concerning the work they carried out, and the need for spiritual renewal. After this event, I crossed the peninsula by train to the city of Seville, near the Atlantic, as I had been invited by Irismenio Ribeiro, a Brazilian missionary, to give a course at a regional theological education centre. I taught this course at Montequinto Baptist Church, pastored by Stella Maris Merlo, an Argentinian missionary who has been involved in evangelism and discipleship in Spain for thirty years. A volunteer from El Salvador, Gladys, provided our meals, one of many Latin American immigrants who volunteer at Spanish churches. These persons are not imperial agents but missionaries from below, as in the New Testament. Glory to the Lord for the missionary vision and practice from young churches who have caught the vision.

3: BAPTISTS: THEOLOGY AND LIFE

In this brief reflection, I will focus on Baptist life as it has been revealed in missionary practice and in the life of Peruvian churches, rather than in theological manuals. None of the missionaries who established Baptist work in Peru were noteworthy thinkers or theologians, and none of them wrote any reference books. The Peruvian Baptists who have written theological reflections have done this mainly as evangelical thinkers, rather than specifically as Baptist theologians. This is not to say that the missionaries had no theology. For example, the first missionaries, such as David Oates, Robert Harris and Randall Sledge, were good biblical expositors and the same can be said of the Argentine pastor, Antonio Gamarra, and the Peruvian, Alejandro Tuesta. Each of them had a strong evangelistic conviction so that their preaching, and all their activity, was aimed at challenging people to place their faith in Jesus Christ as Lord and personal Saviour.

These founders revealed, in their practice, their conviction concerning the human need for salvation and a vibrant faith in Jesus Christ which needed to be communicated to everyone. Likewise, their preaching reflected a deep respect for biblical authority and a theological conviction about the primacy of the Word of God over human traditions. For this reason, their sermons reflected long hours of preparation and concentrated on the exposition of the biblical text. Their sermons were not motivational talks or tales about their experiences, but an attempt to bring to light what the biblical text affirms. I need to emphasise that *the theology of those who founded the Baptist work was reflected in their evangelistic practice and their teaching* in churches, rather than in speeches or writings in academic theology. This theology was also reflected in the *church covenants* of the congregations they planted and in the *hymns,* which were an important part of the emerging churches.

These Peruvian Baptist founders conveyed this theological principle with clarity and conviction to the first generation of Peruvian Baptists. With apologies for the personal example, I need to point out that before being baptised, I had to study the booklet, *Lo que creen los Bautistas* (What Baptists Believe), so that my baptism was a consequence of my convictions regarding the principles of the church I was joining. I also need to point out that my conviction regarding the importance of the Bible was part of my experience growing up in the *Iglesia Evangélica Peruana* (Peruvian Evangelical Church) where I took advantage of biblical exposition in sermons and in books. The openness fostered by my Sunday School teachers in Arequipa led me to read books by theologians, such as John A. Mackay. As a university student bombarded by Marxist propaganda, I had questions regarding my faith for which Baptist textbooks by Carroll, Meyer or Mullins held no answers. In the University Biblical Circle, which I belonged to alongside evangelicals from other denominations, we were forced to develop our own apologetic in the face of Marxism and existentialism. This led to the essays published in my book, *Diálogo entre Cristo y Marx* (*Dialogue between Christ and Marx*), which my Presbyterian colleague, Pedro Arana, published for use among university students during the In-Depth Evangelism campaign.

Baptist Theology

I found the following convictions, which the missionaries emphasised in their teaching and practice, particularly attractive: *the baptism of adult believers*, the *democratic government of the church*, the need for pastoral ministry, the autonomy of the local congregation, stewardship and the financial self-sufficiency of churches. These convictions take us to specific Baptist theological principles and practices. The missionaries not only taught these truths but also sought that the churches they planted put them into practice. Nonetheless, this led to a problem regarding the relationship between theology and practice. Many of the first members of Baptist churches, such as Ebenezer in Miraflores (organised in August 1951) and the First Baptist Church of Lima (organised in November 1952), were believers from other denominations who brought different ideas concerning church life to those taught by the missionaries. That meant that although churches adopted covenants and doctrinal statements which reflected Baptist convictions, some of their members were not fully convinced regarding Baptist practices, especially concerning the idea of a democratic government or the autonomy of the local congregation. The idea that all the members of the church participated in church government, and not a select group of elders or a council, led to problems as people were not used to it. This was worsened by the lack of a national democratic culture and the tendency to rely on charismatic, strong-handed leaders. For others, their monetary offerings followed the Catholic pattern of almsgiving rather than being part of an integral stewardship. For some, the lack of an episcopal body with oversight and authority over local congregations was a problem.

The guiding theological principle was that the New Testament description of the practice of the primitive church should be the norm for the life of our churches here and now. Although different practices, such as baptism by aspersion rather than immersion, infant baptism, the existence of presbyteries and synods, and the authority of bishops, might seem respectable, they lacked biblical foundation. This theological principle is present in a book written for Latin America by a missionary who spent his life in Colombia. In the first chapter he raises the issue: "The primitive church we read about in the New Testament does not have a special name. Yet, probably all churches insist that they descend from this primitive church. How is it possible that there are such different interpretations of the words of Christ, Paul and other writers? We will consider the series of stages through which other groups arrived at erroneous beliefs and practices."[1]

Arguably, all evangelicals will claim that the New Testament is the foundation of their church and denomination. Nonetheless, Baptists have been most insistent that the organisation and practice of their churches must be according to the New Testament model without making concessions to subsequent historical developments. This is connected to the principle that only those who are able to make a confession of their faith (adults or those able to exercise their rational faculties) should be baptised. The historian, William Estep, reminds us that contemporary Baptists have the Anabaptists of the 16th century as their antecedent and affirms that "while Biblical authority was the most important distinction between the reformers and the Catholics, believer's baptism was the most notable distinction between the reformers and Anabaptists. This was, for Anabaptists, the logical consequence of the Reformation principle of *Sola Scriptura*. The more that the Anabaptist movement became distinguishable within the context of the Reformation, the issue of believer's baptism became more valued. The first Anabaptist leaders recognised, without exception, the importance of Baptism ... The first Anabaptist discussions and confessions granted believer's baptism great importance. For this reason, it is unjustifiable to minimise the place of baptism in the life of 16th century Anabaptists; rather a correct interpretation of the role of baptism in Anabaptist life is essential to correctly interpret Anabaptist understanding of discipline and the church."[2]

This same theological principle leads to the Baptist insistence on the separation between Church and State. It is important to remember that Europe, at the time of the 16th century Reformation, had inherited the Christendom concept of the union between Empire and State, between civil and religious power. Within this order, infant baptism was a means to become a member not only of the church but also of the imperial order. In questioning infant baptism, the Anabaptists were also questioning the alliance between empire and church, leading some of them, such as the Mennonites, to adopt a radical pacifism. As Christ rejected violence, therefore the one who recognised Christ as their only Lord and is a true disciple does not place oneself at the command of Caesar, the emperor, to kill others on behalf of the imperial order. Thomas Helwys' book, *A*

---

[1] James E. Giles, *Esto creemos los bautistas* (Santo Domingo: Casa Bautista de Publicaciones (CBP), 1980), 7.
[2] W.R. Estep, *Revolucionarios del siglo XVI. Historia de los anabautistas* (Santo Domingo: CBP, 1975), Chapter 9.

Short Declaration of the Mystery of Iniquity, in which he writes to the King in 1612 requesting religious freedom, has the famous sentence, "Listen oh King and do not despise this advice from the poor ... the King is a mortal man, and not God, therefore he hath no power over the mortal soul of his subjects to make laws and ordinances for them and to set spiritual Lords over them." Helwys died in prison in 1616, as did other defenders of religious freedom. These days, there are some Catholics who opt for a separation between Church and State but in a country like Peru, where the census points to Catholics being a majority, the dominant church still tries to hold on to the economic and social advantages of the union between Church and State, which has been a characteristic of Peru since the Spanish conquest.

Theology for Today

Peruvian Baptists must take into account new factors concerning the theology and practice of their churches in this second decade of the 21st century. I do not believe that the current task is to insist on the Baptist principles which I have mentioned in such a way as to isolate themselves from fundamental Christian theology. In this sense, it is important to pay attention to a theologian such as Justo Anderson who, in identifying Baptist principles, orders them in terms of importance. As a mission theologian who worked for many years in Latin America, Anderson formulates seven principles: the *Christological* principle centres on the Lordship of Christ; the *biblical* principle centres on the authority of the New Testament; the *ecclesiastical* principle is based on a regenerated membership; the *sociological* principle concerns the democratic order in the church; the *spiritual* principle concerns religious freedom; the *political* principle is about the separation between Church and State; and the *evangelistic* principle centres on personal evangelism and the missionary enterprise.[3]

It is important to emphasise that the Christological principle comes first in this sequence as the confession of Jesus as Lord and Saviour is the foundation of our faith. This principle regulates the other principles. If we do not have a clear theology concerning Christ, our practice will fail and we will have no message. We believe in Christ as truly human and truly God. As we believe in the humanity of Christ, we have, for example a model of discipleship and pastoral work. To deny the humanity of Christ is a heresy condemned in the Word (1 John 4:1–3), as is to deny his deity. Even though there are many fundamental differences between Catholics and Evangelicals, it is important to remember that they share this foundational Christological faith and in this sense differ from

---

[3] A new commemorative edition of Justo Anderson's classic work has been released. Justo Anderson, *Historia de los Bautistas* (El Paso: Mundo Hispano, 2015). These principles are mentioned in the second section of the first part of the book, 37-85.

Mormons and Jehovah Witnesses. It is important to make sure that we understand this foundation and know in whom we have believed. A clear Christology leads to clarity in other doctrines, such as the Trinity. A biblical Christology goes hand-in-hand with a Trinitarian confession of faith, because, as we affirm in our doxologies and final benedictions, we believe in the grace of Christ, the love of the Father and the fellowship of the Holy Spirit.

How does this theological principle provide us with discernment to answer some contemporary questions? How can it help us to understand the contemporary situation? As an example, we can look at contemporary debates over our form of worship and the types of songs we should use in our congregations. If we review popular songs by composers such as Marcos Witt and other popular charismatic composers, we see they never make any reference to Jesus's humanity, only his deity. For this reason, they offer a spiritualistic rather than biblical adoration. This is a heretical, docetic hymnology. For the same reason, it uses the militaristic, warrior language of the Old Testament. If there is no reference to the humanity of Jesus, we have no example to follow, no model to propose. The issue of the lyrical content of songs is more important than that of rhythm and instruments. This complete absence of Christ's humanity is a heresy, just as it is heretical to forget Christ's expiatory death and resurrection, and transform him into a guerrilla, as in a certain hymn sung in Sandinista Nicaragua. Hymns are a confession of the faith of God's people; they are sung theology and should be good theology. Paying attention to this principle should lead our musicians to sing or compose hymns which reflect the fullness of the truth concerning Christ and not an escapist spiritualisation.

Church growth provides another example. We all admire churches which grow numerically and would love to see every Baptist church growing, reaching more people with the Gospel. Some take Pentecostal and charismatic churches as their model and claim that Baptist churches should forget the democratic principle and have authoritarian pastors who impose their programme and style on the church according to divine revelation. They claim that this will enable us to grow. Should we sacrifice Biblical principles for efficacy? The problem is that Jesus's example (Luke 22:24–27), and the teaching of Paul (1 Thessalonians 2:3–9) and Peter (1 Peter 5:1-4), offer us a model of pastoral leadership based on service and not of authoritarian leadership. There are pastors who have adopted an authoritarian style of leadership without seeing their churches grow. In Peru, and in other countries, we have seen the dramatic moral failure of abusive charismatic leaders who lacked a system to moderate their style and provide safeguards to the corruption that comes from excessive power.

What criteria should we use to discern whether the Holy Spirit is responsible for the tremendous numerical and financial growth of certain churches, or if it is a consequence of religious manipulation, such as that of popular Catholic religiosity of years gone by? The criteria are theological, or more specifically, Christological. Christ taught us that the work of the Holy Spirit is to glorify Christ, reminding us of his fullness, convincing the world of its need for Christ and make us more similar to Christ. If there is evidence in these growing churches of a fruit which is people and congregations growing continuously in the likeness of Christ, displaying love, a spirit of service and the holiness of life in Christ, then it is clear that the Holy Spirit is at work there. God builds up his church through his Word in the power of the Holy Spirit.

If we lose our rich Baptist theological inheritance, we will become churches without identity or religious clubs which prolong traditions and entertain people. If we deepen our rich heritage, we will be able to answer the new questions which are emerging this century. For example, a close reading of the New Testament reveals that the contemporary rediscovery of the concept of a cell church, the ministry of small groups, has biblical roots. Baptists desire to be biblically democratic and for this they need to be educated in the truth, not becoming blind people passively led by daring dictatorial leaders. As Baptists, we should be a people redeemed by Christ, a community of people who have been regenerated and are the light of the world, and salt of the earth, who *look to the future with hope and practice love because their faith has a firm foundation.*

I would like to end this reflection with a brief reference to four theologians, with books in Spanish, who can allow us to establish the foundations of our evangelical and Baptist faith and deepen its meaning. Bernard Ramm from the United States; the Puerto Rican, Orlando Costas; the Spaniard, José Grau; and René Padilla from Ecuador; all are well-known and appreciated among evangelicals. I have had the privilege of meeting each one personally, and am a witness of their Baptist militancy, and although they have reached wider fame in the Protestant and evangelical world, they were all active members of their local churches. All four have the gift of clarity in their writing and exposition.

Bernard Ramm (1916–1992) was a professor at Eastern Baptist Seminary and other university theological institutions, and active in Baptist churches in the north of the United States. Casa Bautista published his *Diccionario de Teología Contemporánea* (*Dictionary of Contemporary Theology*), a brief but very useful book for understanding basic theological concepts. With regards to the foundation of our faith, I consider the best exposition to be that which Ramm offers in his book, *Special Revelation and the Word of God* (Grand Rapids: Eerdmans, 1961), which I often use in my classes on contemporary theology. According to my students in Madrid, it is possible to download the Spanish version online. Ramm reflects on the centrality of faith in a God who wants to reveal himself to human beings and does that through his general revelation in creation, and through his special revelation that we have in the Scriptures of the Old Testament and the New Testament, the centre being Jesus Christ.

The Spaniard, José Grau (1931–2014), had a lengthy teaching ministry in his own Baptist church in Barcelona and in various evangelical theological institutions. His classical work, the two volume *Catolicismo Romano,* is the most complete work on Catholicism by a Spanish-speaking evangelical writer. He was director of Ediciones Evangélicas Europeas in Barcelona. He published didactic books for those wishing to start their theological reflection in a collection called

A Course in Evangelical Theological Formation, in which two of his books stand out, *Introducción a la Teología* (Barcelona: CLIE, 1973) and *Escatología,* an exposition of Biblical teaching on the second coming which provides an excellent evangelical critique of dispensationalism. *El Fundamento Apostólico* 2nd edition (Bogata: Ediciones Peregrino, 2013) reflects on the biblical foundation of our faith and explains the basis of our confidence in the Bible for our theology and our life.

René Padilla has lived for many decades in Buenos Aires where he was pastor at La Lucila Evangelical Baptist Church and is currently director of Ediciones Kairos, which has published over a hundred books by Latin American evangelical authors. He became widely known due to his excellent speech at the Lausanne World Evangelisation Congress (1974). His book, *Mission Between the Times* (Carlisle: Langham Monographs, 2010), reflects on the time of his theological exploration in Latin America in the years which succeeded the Lausanne Congress. He develops basic themes, such as 'What is the Gospel?', 'The Gospel and Culture', contextualization, and the social dimension of missionary work with depth and clarity.

Orlando Costas (1942–1987) was born in Puerto Rico and grew up in the United States. As pastor of a Spanish-speaking church in Minneapolis, he personally experienced the discrimination against the Spanish-speaking minority. He became a missionary in Costa Rica, working on In Depth Evangelism, in a life of intense activism and reflection. His book, *Christ Outside the Gate* (Maryknoll: Orbis, 1982), is a systematic and creative exposition of his theology of Christian mission. On his return to the United States, he developed the concept of mission from the periphery, reflecting on the significance of the fact that Jesus started his ministry in Galilee. His thought is of special importance now that African, Asian and Latin American Baptists are starting to send missionaries to Muslim countries and Europe, now that mission is coming from the periphery.

IMB missionary, David Oates, and family

Cuban pastor Agüero blessing the marriage of Jacob Padilla and Ruth Escobar

First generation of Peruvian Baptist pastors.
D. Trigoso, F. Cárdenas, C. García, R. Moreno

Missionary Ledford blessing the marriage of
Samuel Escobar and Lilly Artola

General Ronald Román Caballero leading a service

Evangelism-in-Depth, Chiclayo Baptist Church, 1967

PART THREE

Biographical Sketches

4: BLESSED PEACEMAKERS

Two recent news items, one from the secular press and the other from evangelical news outlets, had reminded me of Jesus's words: "blessed are the peacemakers". The first was a photograph of the former president of the United States, Jimmy Carter, who was wearing a bright, large, loose shirt, known as a 'guayabera', while visiting Cuba. The second announced the death of Dr Gustavo Parajón, a doctor known in Nicaragua and Latin America. The news items attracted my attention as I knew both were Baptists, and I know from my little experience how difficult it was to be a peacemaker, starting in one's own home and much more on an international level. Carter and Parajón have been peacemakers, constructors of peace. It was worth reflecting on this theme, writing while Spain went through a tense and strained electoral process during an economic crisis.

The Peace-Making President

When the former president received the Nobel Peace Prize, I went to a bookstore to find a biography of Carter, or some book he had written. The bookstore owner looked at me with a mixture of curiosity and surprise and soon searched his computer. No, there was nothing available. Such was my naivety, I forgot that men of Carter's moral stature appear for a brief moment in the headlines and little more. If it were the latest American writer of shoddy literature, the autobiography of an actress or the latest self-help book on how to become a millionaire, it would soon be translated from English into Spanish to be published a few weeks after being released in the United States. However, Carter did not provide material to interest those editors for whom publishing was a good business. The sad thing was that if I went to the nearest Christian bookstore, I would have the same problem, as what I would find were numerous books on demonology, 19th century classics and lengthy eschatological novels. The biography of a Sunday school teacher who also became president of his country did not seem to attract the attention of evangelical editors. Though admittedly, around twenty years ago, El Paso's Casa Bautista published Carter's book, *Why not the Best?* (Nashville: Broadman Press, 1975), in Spanish, *Por qué no lo mejor.*

One of the things that I most liked about Carter is that since he was young, he was a faithful Sunday School teacher and continued even into his eighties. He was not one of those politicians who had become an evangelical to gain votes. I have in my office two books in English by Jimmy Carter. One is *The Personal Beliefs of Jimmy Carter*,[1] a collection of two of his books, *Living Faith* (1996) and *Sources of Strength* (1997). Sadly, none of those books have been translated into Spanish. My readers will recollect that Carter was president of the United States from 1977 to 1981. In these books, Carter explained with simplicity the Christian faith and provided snippets of his life to illustrate his message. The books displayed his ability to speak simultaneously about doctrine and life, theory and practice, with the quality of a good Sunday school teacher, which Carter had been for many years. The other book is called, *The Blood of Abraham: Perspectives on the Middle East*,[2] and was the fruit of many years of study and reflection. The book was an effort to understand the complex reality of the Middle East. It provided a chronology of the region, starting nine thousand years before Christ until 1985, and had five excellent maps which included Abraham's journey, the establishment of the state of Israel and the situation in 1984.

The book's intention was clear. Carter desired that his readers comprehend such a complex social, economic and political situation, hearing the voices of the different countries participating in the conflicts: Israel, Syria, Lebanon, the Palestine, Jordan, Egypt and Saudi Arabia. There is a chapter dedicated to each country. Carter and his wife travelled to each of these countries, interviewed authorities, listened to representative intellectuals, read reports and observed the daily life of people. One of the things which Carter did after leaving the presidency of his country was to create the Carter Centre at Emory Methodist University in 1982. This is a non-profit, non-partisan organisation which seeks to resolve conflicts, promote democracy, preventing plagues and other afflictions. After Carter travelled throughout the Middle East, the Carter Centre organised an international consultation to analyse the political, social and military situation in the region. The consultation was organised to hear representative voices from each of the countries mentioned.

Anyone who has made the effort to help two parties resolve a conflict knows how important it is to hear both sides. Yet, this is not always easy. As far as possible, the peacemaker needs to remain neutral. Otherwise they would not manage to get both sides to listen to one another. Carter's book, *The Blood of Abraham*, was a clear effort in this direction. In chapter six of *Living Faith*, Carter narrated how after losing his re-election campaign, he desired to return to his private life but decided to start a new career and founded the Carter Centre, along with his wife, Rosalyn. As president, Carter had started the peace-making process in the Middle East, known as Camp David, and he expresses his frustration that his efforts to continue the process with the Palestinians, Jordan

---

[1] New York: Three Rivers Press, 1998.
[2] Boston: Houghton Mifflin Harcourt, 1985.

and Syria had been almost completely abandoned by his successor, the actor, Ronald Reagan. Carter wrote, "my hope was that in some way, I could use my knowledge and experience to occupy myself with this and other world conflicts, and that with Washington's approval, possibly Rosalyn and I could intervene with some mediation efforts. From the start of the 1980s, our visits to the Middle East always received official support and I always presented full reports to the Secretary of State and the White House. On some occasions, I also secretly met with Palestinian leaders".[3]

One of Carter's biographers, Rod Troester, studied Carter's career since he left the presidency, and the title of his book was eloquent: *Jimmy Carter as Peacemaker: A Post Presidential Biography* (1996). Troester reminded us that Carter had been called "the best former president of the United States" and his presidency "was characterised by an emphasis on human rights, humanitarian causes and negotiation rather than confrontation".[4] Carter himself acknowledged in *Living Faith* how difficult it was to take decisions when one was in a position of power, which he once occupied. He told how in the last fourteen months of his presidency, his desire for peace was put to the test by two situations. The first was the Soviet invasion of Afghanistan, seeking to advance towards Pakistan and Iran, then soon after the revolution against the Shah in Iran, when Ayatollah Khomeini's revolutionaries invaded the United States embassy in November 1979 and took sixty-six Americans as hostages.

From all sides, Carter was under pressure to use force to free the hostages and he wrote, "we seriously considered the use of force, which would have been very popular and easy to order. However, I was concerned that if we punished Iran in this fashion, the hostages would be treated with brutality and murdered". Carter decided to send serious warnings to Iran through various private channels and applied economic sanctions. In April 1980, there was an unsuccessful rescue attempt. Carter wrote, "finally, through intense negotiations during the last three days and nights of my presidency, when I was unable to sleep at all, we managed to achieve our proposed objectives. At ten in the morning on 20th of January 1981, the refugees were on a plane at Tehran Airport waiting to abandon Iran … I met them at Wiesbaden Airport in Germany".[5]

A few lines later, Carter wrote: "I have had to face physical danger, financial crises, political failure and doubts about my career. In all these crises, self-analysis, self-questioning and prayer have been at the centre of my focus. Here, prayer has been the most essential. Even when I have decided not to share my problems with another human being, not even Rosalyn, I have always managed to share them with God. Prayer helps me to understand the problem I am facing

---

[3] *The Personal Beliefs*, 135-136.
[4] Santa Barbara: Praeger, 1996, 3.
[5] *The Personal Beliefs*, 103.

and understand myself, even those things which are buried in the deepest part of my being. This starts an important healing process."[6] As is widely known, Carter received the Nobel Peace Prize in October 2002.

The Peace-Making Missionary

Although on a different scale, the story of the Nicaraguan Baptist doctor, Gustavo Parajón, is another example of a peace-making career in the agitated Central American environment. From 1936 to 1979, the Somoza family governed Nicaragua, truly owning lives and farms. Since its independence from Spain in 1821, Nicaragua has a long history of commercial relations with Great Britain and the United States, and internal conflicts between conservative politicians and liberals. Some episodes seem to come out of a soap opera. Dr Parajón recalls one such event in a consultation dedicated to evangelicals and the political power in Latin America: "In 1855, William Walker, a lawyer, adventurer and filibuster from the south of the United States, arrived in Nicaragua, invited by liberals to help in the fight against the conservatives. As bold as brass, William Walker, along with his filibustering accomplices, declared himself president of Nicaragua, established slavery and received immediate diplomatic recognition from the United States. William Walker confiscated the Cornelius Vanderbilt company, which belonged to a millionaire from the United States who joined the effort of other Central American companies and England to get rid of Walker. A Honduran firing squad executed Walker when a British naval officer captured him and handed him over to the Honduran army."[7] The presence of marine troops from the United States was a constant feature of the history of Nicaragua until 1933. The marines created the National Guard, a military force whose officers were all marines; that is, elite troops. They made Anastasio Somoza leader of the National Guard and in 1934, he secured complete military and political power in Nicaragua. It was in this manner that he and his family remained in power until 1979.

Gustavo Parajón was son of Arturo Parajón, one of the first Nicaraguan Baptist pastors.[8] Gustavo studied medicine and received a scholarship to graduate at Harvard University. He married Joan Morgan in the United States and they returned in 1968 as missionaries of the American Baptist Churches (North) for Gustavo to work as a doctor. Gustavo begun as a doctor at the Nicaraguan Baptist Hospital, but becoming aware of the acute needs of the rural

---

[6] Ibid., 104.
[7] Gustavo A. Parajón, "Estructura de poder en Nicaragua", in Pablo Deiros, *Los evangélicos y el poder político* (Grand Rapids; Nueva Cración, 1986), 237.
[8] Parajón's biographical details are taken from Stan Slade, 'Central America Celebrates Gustavo Parajón', in *International Ministries Update,* November 2006, 1-2.

population which could not be treated at the hospital, Gustavo founded PROVADENIC, an organisation to assist in the prevention of diseases through hygiene and the fight against malnutrition.

When an earthquake shook the capital city of Managua in 1972, 40,000 homes were destroyed and 200,000 were left homeless. It was necessary to face the catastrophe and Gustavo challenged the evangelical population and with the help of eight churches, founded CEPAD (The Evangelical Committee to Aid Victims).[9] They sought to use the funds that came from neighbouring countries and the United States with transparency and effectiveness. This became well-known in Nicaragua and their honest administration earned the population's respect, in contrast to the inefficient and corrupt way in which the Samoza administration administered the massive funds which came from overseas. In 1973, CEPAD changed its last name in its title to 'development' as its main focus was no longer on victims, but on cooperating with long-term development projects not only in Managua, but throughout the country. The specific areas of focus were education, the development of human resources, rural development, regional development along the Atlantic coast, the creation of a pastoral studies centre and relationships with churches. In this way, CEPAD became, in practical terms, a kind of national council of evangelical churches.[10]

Opposition grew in the face of the totalitarian and corrupt Somoza policies and soon took the form of the Sandinista Front for National Liberation. CEPAD's legal status gave it credibility with the government but its personnel in rural areas were witnesses of the atrocities committed by the National Guard in its fight against the Sandinistas. "In April 1977, CEPAD's Pastoral Committee received from many brethren, especially Pentecostals from the northern zone of the country, documentary evidence of the murder of evangelicals, men, women and children by the National Guard. After receiving the report and deliberating over its contents, the Assembly decided that three members would seek to talk with Anastasio Somoza Debayle (grandson of the founder of the dynasty) on behalf of CEPAD to denounce these murders and demand, in the name of God, the end of these atrocities."[11]

One can say, to summarise a lengthy and painful process that lasted through the 1970s, that the Sandinista revolution was successful. However, Somoza's supporters organised themselves as a movement to harass the new Sandinista government and this movement, known as La Contra, received support from the United States. According to the North American missionary, Stan Slade, "When

---

[9] Data about CEPAD can be found in "Breve historia del CEPAD", Deiros, *Los Evangélicos y el Poder Político*, 331-341.
[10] Currently CEPAD stands for Council of Evangelical Churches for Denominational Alliance and is a representative organism for Nicaraguan evangelicals.
[11] "Breve historia del CEPAD" in Deiros, op. cit., 335.

the Sandinista revolution defeated the dictator, Anastasio Somoza Debayle, in June 1979, CEPAD's rural development projects had been functioning for years in all of rural Nicaragua. Thus, when La Contra's war, supported by the United States, started soon after, CEPAD was one of the few organisations which had the presence and credibility in rural zones where the battles took place, and at a national level. This gave CEPAD a strategic position to identify the abuses by both parties to oppose them, and also work for reconciliation between both sides."[12]

In 1981, the American Baptists (North) granted Parajón the Dahlberg Peace Award because even before the La Contra war had begun, he already had a solid reputation for his work in favour of peace, justice and reconciliation. Nonetheless, as the Reagan government supported La Contra, its propaganda in the United States slandered the Sandinista government and invented charges against it. Many Baptist citizens in the United States did not know whether to believe their own government or their missionary from Nicaragua who provided a different version of events.[13] For the Parajón couple, these were years of trial and conflict. Correspondence between Carter and Parajón can be found from those days. According to Slade, "During this period, Parajón followed the counsel of the New Testament in a deeper way. When Jesus announced his blessing upon the peace-makers in the Sermon on the Mount, he immediately proceeded to speak about those who were persecuted, slandered and accused because of justice (Mt 5:9-12). Jesus knew that working for peace brought slander and condemnation from those who wanted to win at any cost without concern for the truth." In 2006, the Baptist World Alliance granted Parajón its Human Rights award and both his own country, and the Central American Parliament, gave him medals as a distinguished citizen. His wife, Joan, is known in Nicaragua for her humanitarian work among prisoners and is famous for the choir she has formed in prisons.

I give thanks to God for the testimony of these Baptist leaders and their wives. They were faithful not only as a Sunday School teacher in one case, pastor and social activist in the other, but they were also valuable instruments of peace. Blessed peacemakers! It seems to me that in Spain and Latin America, we lack people with this vocation. When one participates in Spanish and Latin American Baptist contexts, it becomes clear that there are many situations of conflict that could be solved if there were more peacemakers. Carter and Parajón have given us a good example of this on a much greater scale.

---

[12] Slade, op. cit., 2.
[13] A detailed and well documented account of this conflict can be read in Raymond P. Jennings op. cit., 306-314.

5: THE IRREPROACHABLE GENERAL

A visitor to the First Baptist Church of Lima would hardly have suspected that the enthusiastic choir director was a General of the Peruvian police, and that early Monday morning he would be behind his desk in his office at DERIVE, the police department responsible for stolen vehicles in the capital of Peru. Ronald Román Caballero exerted both activities, on Sunday and on Monday, with the same effort, dedication and discipline. Ronald was one of the lay Baptist brothers who would sing their faith with enthusiasm and dedication on Sunday, and on Monday would live out their faith in the same way.

Ronald was born in Huancayo, in Peru's central mountain range, and was one of those extroverts that are a pleasure to talk to due to the way they communicate their enthusiasm and their love of life. From a young age, he loved music and learnt to play the guitar. In 1952, he sat the entrance exam and joined what was then Peru's School of Officers for the Police. In 1954, when Tacna was reincorporated into Peru, many military institutions and national schools for men and women sent delegations, including their standard bearers and escorts. Ronald travelled as an escort for the School of Officers and Lucila Roberta Diaz Rojas, known as Tita, travelled with the Mercedes Cabello National School. From the meeting between Ronald and Tita, a romance blossomed which would lead to marriage when he completed his studies and entered active service as a police officer. This was the beginning of an exemplary family which God blessed with four daughters and a son, and would play an important role in the life of Peruvian Baptists.

As with any police officer, Ronald Román had to travel wherever his police bosses would send him, such as different cities in Peru. He started working in Lima then, as a Lieutenant, he was sent to his hometown of Huancayo where he was well-known, particularly for his passion for music. He would rehearse in his home, along with his friend, the tenor, Eduardo Cárdenas, and other musicians and singers. This group adopted the native name Karamanduka and became well-known on Huancayo radio and television. Ronald and Tita were faithful Catholics and thus, followed church rites in their marriage, continuing with the birth of their children. In Huancayo, Ronald started to come closer to Christ, being invited by his friend, Pascual Cárdenas, to visit the temple of the Assemblies of God.

Ronald experienced a spiritual emptiness and read considerably; in his search for books with Pascual, he started to read the Bible. He gave his life to Christ in September 1963. In April 1964, Ronald travelled with Tita, his three daughters and new-born son to Chiclayo, where he had been transferred after being promoted to captain. In his new role, he was surprised to discover other colleagues in the Civil Guard who were believers and kept a Bible in the police office. Eventually, Ronald encountered the Baptist church which, at this time, was pastored by David Trigoso, who gave the family a warm welcome. The pastor's father, Vicente Trigoso Pinto, had been a sergeant in the police and had known Christ in Cusco. In Arequipa, he shared the Gospel with his colleague and friend, the constable, Juan Escobar Peña, father of the author of these lines.

With a deep pastoral perception, Pastor David Trigoso became aware of Ronald and Tita's gifts and dedication, and they started to collaborate actively in the life of the church, especially in the Sunday School, studying in the Preparation Union. In September 1964, their last daughter was born and in December, Ronald and Tita were baptised in the Reque river. That same day, sister Tita was bitten by some insects which caused a terrible infection in her left leg. They attempted to heal this through their own efforts, later turning to doctors, but the leg became increasingly worse and was on the verge of being amputated. In despair, Ronald believed that God had abandoned him and wanted nothing more to do with Him but at this time, his brother in Christ, the junior officer, César López and his wife, Luisa, helped him to renew his faith in Christ and counselled the couple to pray and read the Bible continuously, using natural remedies in their treatment. The Lord responded with the complete healing of the leg and the spiritual life of the couple. As they had fallen into debt and were unable to pay their rent, a Christian family, Vásquez Chuqui, allowed them to live in an empty house they owned at no cost.

The In-Depth Evangelism campaign was held in Peru in 1967 as part of an effort by all evangelical churches to proclaim the Gospel and gain new disciples for Christ. Ronald participated in these campaigns forming duos, trios and quartets. In 1968, the family returned to Lima and became members of the First Baptist Church in Lima, where Ronald was able to develop his musical knowledge, piano-playing and conducting a choir. Both at work and at church, Ronald would set high targets and would work intensively to achieve what he wanted. Thus, in 1970, already a major and police superintendent in the city of Piura, he organised the United Choir formed of Baptists, Nazarenes and Pentecostals. In 1972, he formed a choir at Emmanuel Baptist Church in Chiclayo which participated in evangelistic campaigns, radio and television programmes.

Different forms of adversity affected the Román family on various occasions. The initial impact would shake Ronald's life and test his faith in God and Jesus Christ but soon, with the support of his wife, he would manage to withstand and overcome the crisis. Thus, in 1972, when the family were being moved to Chiclayo, they packed all their belongings in a large lorry belonging to a friend.

Ronald and Tita were at a farewell meeting organised by their church in Piura. The meeting was interrupted when a fellow Christian in the fire brigade gave them the news that the lorry with all their belongings had caught fire and although there were no human victims, all the family's belongings had been burnt. Tita recalls seeing Ronald shaken by the impact of the tragedy, sit down and look crestfallen. After a few minutes of silence and anguish, he stood up and made the words of the patriarch, Job, his own, stating them in a loud voice, "the Lord gave, the Lord took away, blessed be the name of the Lord" (Job 1:21). Having gone through this trial, they felt the hand of God blessing them in many forms. They received shelter for forty-five days at the home of Sergeant Murrugarra and his wife, Yolanda Villasís. They received donations from Christians and friends all over Peru, having more than they could imagine. In 1974, Ronald was affected by a disease to his vocal chords which left him unable to speak or sing. So, he sought other ways to worship the Lord, learning the accordion, the mandolin and the banjo. From approximately 1975 to 1998, he directed the choir of the First Evangelical Baptist Church in Lima.

In a country such as Peru, where corruption spreads its tentacles throughout politics and public as administration, Ronald had the Christian honour and valour to preserve himself incorruptible. He was admired and feared for his rectitude and would often express the integrity of his vocation by affirming "they will never be able to point a finger at me". This was tested in 1988 when Ronald reached the rank of General and was put in charge of DERIVE, the Peruvian police department for stolen vehicles. The role of this department is to prevent, detect, investigate and denounce vehicle theft. Ronald had to face corruption. The Interior Ministry pressurised Ronald to ignore due process when dealing with a transaction involving a stolen vehicle. Ronald refused this request to ignore the law with sincerity and firmness. The response was swift. The boss involved used his influence in the high spheres of the government in power and Ronald was forced into retirement in the same year that he had been made General, bringing to an end the brilliant career of an honourable man.

Lima's *Oiga* magazine, in its edition on 26th December 1988, published a column describing the events with the title "How to demoralize the police." The following commentary appears beneath a photo of Ronald. "General Ronald Román Caballero of the Police Force was forced into retirement for the sole 'offence' of trying to reorganise his department and facing up to government protégés ... the same fate has befallen other honest officials."

Upon his retirement, Ronald was able to state with firmness and conviction, "I leave with my head lifted high." This was recognised by many friends and colleagues who knew his trajectory. Nonetheless, a new opportunity for service in his beloved police force emerged when he was invited to teach as a lecturer at the Police Officers School. One of the subjects he was asked to teach was that of Professional Ethics, which he taught with enthusiasm and authenticity as this reflected what had been his conduct throughout his life as an officer, and not just academic theory.

As a high-ranking police officer and experienced Christian, Ronald worked alongside the pastors of the churches where he and his family were members in the different towns where they were sent to live. He combined professional knowledge with disciplined activism and his opinions were well-respected by his brothers and sisters in the faith. He also wrote articles on his specialist knowledge for the magazine, *Destellos Bautistas.* Herbert García, pastor of the First Baptist Church of Lima in the 1980s, recalls with gratitude the long hours of rest and renewal he spent fishing with Ronald on the beaches of Chorrillos. Ronald was an active participant in the Peruvian Association of Christians in the Military, over which he presided for a while.

Ruth Escobar de Padilla, a leader of the Baptist Women's organisation and activist in church involvement in adult literacy and social services on the outskirts of Lima, and remote towns in the interior of the country, developed a lengthy friendship with the Román family. She worked alongside Tita in various activities with Baptist women at a national, regional and local level. Ruth recalls with gratitude the times when Ronald warned her of the dangers of some of the places where she carried out her projects. She also recalls the occasions when Ronald would accompany her to remote and dangerous places for projects, serving the needs of persons and communities immersed in poverty.

In 1998, Ronald suffered a Progressive Supranuclear Palsy which started to affect his whole body and person. In the following years, God enabled Tita and the family to care for their patient in an exemplary manner. In 2010, Ronald went to the presence of the Lord whom he had served with dedication and enthusiasm. His life reveals that it is possible to be a faithful and active Peruvian Baptist believer and a high-ranking military officer with irreproachable conduct. God's people are called to be light in this way. As Paul affirms, "Do everything without grumbling or arguing, so that you may become blameless and pure children of God without fault in a warped and crooked generation. Then you will shine among them like stars in the sky." (Philippians 2:14-15). Thus, Ronald Román Caballero shone. To God be the glory for his exemplary life.

6: José Cardona's Heritage

One can summarise José Cardona's life and work in the same way one can speak about noteworthy characters in the Bible and in history: he was the right man at the right time. I had the opportunity of meeting him in 1966 when I went to study in Madrid and the Spanish context was starting to change with the possibility of some religious liberty in Franco's Spain. Spanish bishops had fiercely opposed the document on Religious Liberty from the Second Vatican Council, yet the European Union was being developed and it was necessary to change Spain's public image with the potential arrival of many more tourists. The country could not remain as the bishops who, as they still do today, only look to the past. It was at this crucial moment that the Baptist pastor, José Cardona, emerged as a providential figure for evangelicals and Spain itself.

Many pages have been written about Cardona upon his departure to his Father's house. Among those which have touched me, I include the magisterial, humane, kind and cordial description by Juan A. Monroy of his dialogue with his friend in the pages of *Protestante Digital*. Máximo García Ruiz's latest book, *Libertad Religiosa en España* (Religious Liberty in Spain), offers an analytical narrative of the struggle for religious liberty, revealing the value of Cardona's activities. The Acknowledgements include a tribute to José Cardona Gregori who "knew how to empower the struggle for religious liberty, who knew how to lead a project which even those entities who created it did not believe in, who resisted winds and tides, not losing his way due to the many difficulties, or the lack of understanding which was always present, nor the regular confrontations, not even the occasional betrayals, always maintaining as his slogan the defence of religious liberty for all".[1]

I have little to add as I was a friend who only met José during my sporadic visits to Spain. We were together at the Berlin Congress on Evangelism in November 1966. I also visited him a few times with the great Argentinian journalist, Alejandro Clifford, and supported his efforts in the Iberian Evangelisation Congress of 1974. From then onwards, our meetings were brief

---

[1] Máximo García Ruiz, *Libertad Religiosa en España* (Madrid: Consejo Evangélico de Madrid, 2006), 14.

but always left me with that positive fraternal sensation which is only felt by those who love their fellow evangelicals and at times suffer their pain, as the author Unamuno suffered Spain's pain. What I wish to share in these lines is a reflection on certain points which seem to explain the success of the unique ministry carried out by José Cardona and need to be evaluated with historical sensibility, considering the future of Spanish Protestantism. It is my opinion that certain personal characteristics of José Cardona led to his success and can be used to construct an agenda for those called by the Lord to continue his labour in the new religious situation in Spain.

Identity and Openness

Cardona never ceased to be a Baptist pastor. Nonetheless, his responsibility called him to serve all evangelicals. He once commented on some of the surprising discoveries he made as he related with the different expressions of Spanish Protestantism. This was already a complex reality when Cardona started his labour and became even more variegated and diverse as the years went by, and the protection of tolerance, which is not the same as liberty, was initially offered. Without losing his identity, he was guided by a spirit of openness and respect towards all evangelical organisations and denominations that were in Spain, or desired to arrive. His cordiality was united with the prudence and respect thar comes from well-assimilated experience, which was essential in his task of building bridges and seeking to overcome sectarian temptations with mutual respect.

There are evangelicals who believe it is necessary to protect their identity by shutting themselves inside their own expression of Christian faith and avoiding contact and relations with those who are different. Even though they may reluctantly acknowledge a minimum common evangelical denominator, there is no desire to cultivate cameraderie, nor possibility of cooperation with others. At times, when a religious minority faces the need to come together and coincide in the efforts towards a common mission, persons such as Cardona receive the task of developing this closeness, building bridges and ensuring that there is a minimum of mutual respect. We need more and more people who have these gifts and we should pray that God sends this kind of worker to his fields.

Political Sensibility

The struggle for religious liberty in Catholic countries leads evangelicals, sooner or later, to act in the world of politics. I am not talking about party politics or the quest for positions of power. I am referring to the minimum of consciousness as citizens, knowledge of the laws and familiarity with power mechanisms that are required to represent the interests of the evangelical community before the State and the government in power. When the Evangelical Defence Committee was formed in 1956, it needed an executive secretary and José Cardona, a Baptist pastor and Justice Secretary in Denia, was chosen as his background was a significant preparation for the task ahead. A self-respecting Baptist pastor understands democratic practices and a Justice Secretary understands laws, political practices and the corridors of power.

In his didactic narrative of the struggle for religious liberty in Spain, José María Martínez affirms, "slowly Cardona's patience, tact and firmness started to influence the higher spheres of government, which made possible a constructive dialogue, especially in the General Department of Interior Policy and the Foreign Affairs Ministry".[2] These nouns – patience, tact and firmness – are well-chosen. They are indispensable for political activity and negotiations with State administration, a task which also requires knowledge of legislation, familiarity with personalities and characters, and with different contemporary political trends. When facing power, a citizen needs to avoid the extremes of servility and insolence and know how to defend their position from a platform of dignity and awareness of rights.

The political sensitivity and virtues that José Cardona displayed are even more important now that doors are opening to relate to power on all levels, from district councils to ministries. Respect and dialogue do not mean abandoning one's principles or lack of realism. In 1993, Cardona wrote in a somewhat disappointed tone regarding the closed attitude of Spanish bishops towards the theme of religious liberty, "In all these years, I have not received a single word of verbal or written support from the Episcopal Conference of the Catholic Church in Spain. We knew, and still know, that Spanish bishops – with a few specific exceptions – have never been supportive of the State dealing with us. If this initiative (concerning the FEREDE agreement of 1992) had needed to come from Catholic bishops, we would have remained in a clandestine existence for all time."[3]

Diplomatic Ability

Pastor José Cardona was a tireless talker and a restrained, attentive dialogue partner, with a great sense of humour. He had the capacity, which emerges from experience and self-control, to know how to speak, to listen and stay quiet. He was able to see the funny side of things and use humour to diffuse tense situations. Pastor Cardona developed a noteworthy diplomatic ability in his dealings with those in power to seek freedom for his own. When I talk about relating to power, I refer not only to his dealings with Spanish political

---

[2] José M. Martínez, *La España evangélica ayer y hoy* (Barcelona: Clie-Andamio, 1944), 349-350.
[3] José Cardona, *Alternativa 2000*, January-February, 1993, 2, quoted in Martínez, op. cit., 383.

authorities but also his relationships with powerful figures among evangelical leaders. It is necessary to acknowledge that we often meet evangelical leaders who have a certain level of power in their ecclesiastical context but do not always exercise this power according to biblical principles. Máximo García's aforementioned book reveals details of the difficult process of seeking a minimum evangelical consensus to allow for dealings with the political power of the State. In both contexts, José Cardona displayed an exquisite diplomatic genius.

Deep religious convictions create deep roots in our conscience that, on many occasions, lead to discrepancies and exclusions in which the religious dimension makes us intransigent. As a religious minority, evangelicals have survived thanks to their refusal to compromise some of their principles, which has led to martyrdom and marginalisation. New times of liberty require the development, especially among leaders, of the diplomatic ability which Cardona displayed without abandoning one's convictions. It is necessary to listen and consider those who have different positions from our own without immediately adopting a posture of exclusion which closes our eyes and ears to the reality we face. There is a whole art of seeking the minimum consensus which allows common actions which overcome denominational differences and different sectorial interests. Cardona has left as his legacy an example of diplomatic activity.

Love for Evangelicals

When one spoke with Cardona, his love and concern for his fellow evangelicals was obvious. His close friends recognise that during his life, Cardona was in contact with the best and worst of evangelicalism. He did not tire, did not become discouraged, but remained on the inside, doing what was possible. One of the greatest pastoral concerns is the exodus of young people from evangelical churches. It is still necessary to carry out a study of the causes to seek a pastoral remedy for this serious problem. Things can only be changed from the inside. The great missionary challenge of post-modern culture demands evangelicals are able to learn the virtues incarnated by José Cardona. It is necessary to know, take advantage of and be grateful to God for this heritage.

7: TWO BAPTISTS AS GOD DESIRES

Although I wanted to, I was not able to attend the Baptist Centennial celebrations in Birmingham, England. These collective experiences are valuable when we know how to live and value them. I have avidly read the many materials which have come into my hands, have navigated the Baptist World Alliance web page and spoken with those who participated in this spectacular celebration. I would have loved to have renewed my contact with Baptists from Asia, Africa, the Americas and Europe whom I have met during my pilgrimage

I would especially have liked to meet one Baptist personally and renew my friendship with two others. I would say that all three of them are from a good Baptist brew. I would like to have shaken Jimmy Carter's hand, and also spoken with Lauran Bethell, a missionary colleague based in Holland who received a Human Rights Award from the Baptist World Alliance, and with Tony Campolo, a sociologist and colleague at Eastern University where I taught for twenty years. These are two Baptist activists, representative of hundreds of others who are unknown, yet are salt and light in their societies, persons whose presence and witness strengthens our faith.

We invited Lauran Bethell in Valencia to give a course for volunteers in Urban Mission. It was a short course on evangelical work among women trapped in prostitution networks. Lauran is an expert in this field and is currently a consultant for various international organisations. Daughter of an American Baptist pastor, she started her career at an international university that her denomination has in Hong Kong. Feeling she was called into missionary service, she studied theology and upon graduation was commissioned by International Ministries of the American Baptist Churches for service in Thailand. There she encountered the terrible reality of young girls who still being teenagers were sold by their parents, deceived or simply attracted into prostitution. To help the victims of this inhuman commerce, Lauran created the New Life Centre in Chiang Mai in 1987. The Centre offers freedom and hope for women and girls who manage to escape these networks, where they receive literacy, Christian education and artisanal training. There is a very effective rehabilitation programme and an educational programme to reduce the risk of other women becoming victims of this modern plague. This is delicate and risky work in a country where Christians are a miniscule minority in a sea of Buddhism.

For thirteen years, Lauran familiarised herself with the social and economic mechanisms which facilitate this trade in human lives, which is also active in Spain and in the rest of the world. From providing suitable attention to the victims, she began to move towards a deeper knowledge of the causes of prostitution. This familiarity led her to progressively act as a consultant for international organisations involved in the struggle against prostitution networks. She also became aware of many Christians who were dedicated to helping women who were trafficking victims. In 2004, Lauran organised and presided over an International Consultation of Ministries with women in prostitution which had activists from twenty-five countries as participants. Thus, the Christian Alliance regarding Prostitution was founded.

To facilitate her work, Lauran moved for a period to Prague in the Czech Republic where she founded the Hope Project to help gypsy women from Bulgaria who were the victims of trafficking, in collaboration with the European Baptist Federation. Currently she lives in Holland and still maintains contact with the two New Life Centres which still exist in Thailand. Lauran has acquired a vast knowledge of the subject through observation, study and above all practical service so that when the government of the United States wished to pass legislation on human trafficking, Lauran was called to the Senate as an expert and had the opportunity to communicate her sensibility and insight in the service of a very hard cause.

Tall and thin, with great sympathy and cordiality, those who meet Lauran for the first time may not guess her level of determination and bravery. She certainly deserves the award for her struggle in favour of human rights that the Baptist World Alliance gave her, and which she received from Jimmy Carter.

My other colleague and Baptist friend is Professor Tony Campolo, a typical Italian-American from the south of Philadelphia in Pennsylvania. His Italian cultural background overflows when he speak, gestures with both hands and laughs loudly, and when on other occasions he is moved to tears. Tony is a sociologist and has carved out a brilliant career at Eastern University. My children have had him as a teacher and can tell numerous anecdotes which Tony tells his classes. He is a natural speaker, a great teller of stories that one can listen to with pleasure beyond midnight. He is in demand as a professional speaker and has published about twenty books which have an agile style and deal with themes which can be considered hot potatoes, which nobody wants to deal with. From an evangelical perspective, he writes with imagination and courage on topics such as the charismatic movement, homosexuality, music in church services and Christian political activism.

Tony is a critic of some of the so-called tele-evangelists, popular evangelical television preachers, and observes with concern the swing to the right in the political life of evangelicals in the United States; that is the promotion of policies which favour the rich, the white and the large companies to the detriment of common citizens. For this reason, he has been blacklisted by more than one fundamentalist in the United States.

Nonetheless, there is another Tony, possibly less well-known and celebrated. This is the social activist who applies sociology to solve the numerous urban problems in his home city. Campolo has set up schools and service centres for children in the poorest and most forgotten neighbourhoods of Philadelphia. He has used his oratory skills to convince hundreds of young, middle- or upper-class students to volunteer for a month serving the poor in the city. These educational and service projects have opened the eyes of some and encouraged them to explore their vocation, serving in what we can call the urban frontier of the United States, one of the most difficult mission fields in the contemporary world. Tony has earned the respect of politicians, urbanists and journalists. When President Bill Clinton suffered moral failure in a scandalous adultery, he sought pastoral support. Somehow, Tony was discreetly invited to the White House to give pastoral assistance to the president. Tony does not provide many details but is simply grateful to God and believes that he carried out his duty. I give thanks to God for the life and ministry of this activist and popular speaker, and for the good causes he has initiated and defended.

8: OUR FRIEND, MARGARET

Following an earthquake of 8.0 on the Richter scale which afflicted Peru on the 15th August 2007, a generous gift was sent by Spanish Baptists to help Peruvian Baptists provide food for close to 6,000 people who were victims of the earthquake. The following are my notes from Monday, 26th November 2007:

"The aid programme started thirty-six hours after the quake. Pastor Pepe Flores, president of the Peruvian Baptist Convention, in his gratitude for the generous offer which the UEBE sent to Peru, also expressed his thankfulness towards the British Baptists who two years before had sent Margaret Swires to Peru with BMS World Mission, after fifteen years' service in Natal, North-east Brazil. Margaret currently runs the Convention's Family and Social Action Department and puts a unique level of energy into her task. This contagious enthusiasm is essential to attract the support of volunteers who travel once a week to the south of Lima to do an intense labour of service to their neighbours.

My wife, Lilly, and I decided to travel with Margaret on her journey this Monday, 26th November. As we travelled southwards on the South Pan-American Highway, we remembered the years between 1980 and 1985 when Lilly would make the same journey for her ministry among prisoners at the women's jail, and would also take sixty children to the Scripture Union camp at Kawai Beach, located at kilometre 96 of the highway. The two other volunteers travelling with us were Débora Maguiña and her husband, Rubén. All four of us remarked with admiration how Margaret had learnt the art of driving on the streets of Lima and the Pan-American highway. This is certainly not easy for the average European driver as it requires constant attention, great serenity and agility to make the manoeuvres required to respond to unexpected and illogical movements, which are typical of some Peruvian drivers.

Our destination is Chincha, 187 kilometres to the south of Lima, a city located close to the sea in a valley known for agricultural activity. The sun and sandy soil make this region ideal for cultivating certain fruits, vines and asparaguses which are exported to European destinations, including Spain. Chincha was one of the worse-affected cities by the earthquake and Morada de Dios Church in Lima, pastored by the Convention's president, had been establishing evangelistic contacts seeking to plant a church. The other affected cities where the Convention has decided to concentrate its aid efforts for the victims are Pisco and Cañete. The Southern Baptist Mission concentrated its efforts in Ica, another important city affected, whilst other Christian denominations and organisations focused their labour in other zones afflicted by the earthquake.

We left Lima at six-thirty in the morning under an intense fog which followed us for most of our route alongside the Pacific Ocean. Upon arrival in Chincha, three hours later, there was a bright sun which astonished us as it reflected on the sand and dust along the way. In Chincha, Margaret and the team of volunteers distributed four tons of food which had arrived in eighteen soup kitchens. These groups of women cook daily in kitchens which serve about twenty-five families each. The Convention came to the conclusion that considering the precarious nature of the situation, which affected mainly children and old people, and the bureaucratic inefficiency of government aid, feeding the starving was the agenda on which their efforts focused. Initially, it was necessary to register those who would receive the aid and study the best way to purchase and distribute the food. It was decided they should purchase in Chincha, as to bring the food in from Lima would make the process more expensive and more complicated.

The first step by the team of volunteers was to organise themselves. We met César, a young volunteer who lived in Chincha and soon, with Pastor Lucas Maguiña and his son Josué, volunteers who had travelled from Lima by bus. We went to the market, bought the food, hired a lorry and soon travelled to the nine collection points which provided the soup kitchens. The dusty alleys which surrounded the market were a true labyrinth. Margaret drove, evading the left-over fish which remained in the street and the so-called mototaxis – motorcycles converted into tricycles which were able to carry up to three passengers sitting down, and an unbelievable amount of cargo. Margaret left her powerful Volkswagen next to the stall of a Christian lady who ensured thieves did not open the car and take it. Being suspicious is the rule to survive in a world of poverty and delinquency.

Once they had arrived at the market, Margaret and Débora negotiated the purchase of four tons of food amid a swarm of clients and loaders who were in constant movement. The lady running the stall had an incredible negotiating ability but Margaret and Débora were her equals in quality control and haggling, when possible and necessary. After the order was finalised, three loaders started taking the food to the lorry where Pastor Maguiña and his volunteers organised the food for distribution: that week they were taking pea flour, rice, oil, pasta, flour, tuna, milk and sugar. While the lorry was being loaded, Margaret took us to the home of Teresa, a lady interested in the Gospel who had opened her house for meetings and where, when necessary, volunteers could sleep as this home had a luxury, running water for some hours of the day and a functioning toilet.

We returned to the lorry at about midday and the distribution began. These were areas increasingly farther from the city centre, with streets of earth and often without running water or electricity. It was a belt of misery and all over one could see the devastating effects of the earthquake. Families lived in tents of all shapes and sizes, amid fallen walls, weak dogs barking incessantly, and water tanks, occasionally full and occasionally empty. Nonetheless, each soup kitchen we visited was a small warren where half a dozen women of all ages worked with dedication and enthusiasm. The spectacle of those sweaty, smiling women working was a sign of hope, contrasting with their surrounding environment.

Margaret, Débora, César and the other volunteers were greeted with signs of appreciation and respect. Some of the women commented happily about how they enjoyed a special class brought by a young pastor from Lima on the Sunday, who combined his roles as preacher and teacher with a considerable ability as an illusionist and ventriloquist. Some men and teenagers turned up to help unload the lorry but the women were not left out, helping to carry the heavy bags. Débora watchfully monitored the quantities of food and asked the community representative to sign a spreadsheet of what was received. With her indigenous hat, under the strong rays of the midday sun, Margaret talked animatedly with women in her Spanish, which every now and then was tinged with Portuguese words or slang.

Thus, the day's labour progressed and along the way, we were covered with sand and sweat but also full of gratitude to the Lord. At three in the afternoon, we stopped with the group of volunteers to eat at the home of Irma, a community leader with a notable capacity for communication and management. We ate the same as that served in the soup kitchens; potatoes served the Peruvian way with a spicy sauce, and a plate of spaghetti with chicken. Also, which cannot be avoided in this globalised world, something special for the visitors: a glass of Coca-Cola.

Lilly and I returned by bus to Lima as the team of volunteers still had work to do and we needed to go to a meeting at seven in the evening. Arriving in Lima, we travelled through streets and avenues with skyscrapers and bright billboards. This is a major contrast with the poverty we had seen in Chincha that day. Ever since its foundation as a country in which the Spanish and indigenous people intermingled in the 16th century, Peru had been a country of contrasts. At times, it seemed that globalisation made these contrasts even more intense. This is a vast and complex challenge for Christian mission."